MW01534415

Advanced Forex Trading - 3 Hour Crash Course

Learn the Advanced Forex Investing Strategies the Professionals Use to Make Life Changing Money

Edward Day

© Copyright 2020 - All rights reserved.

The content contained within this book may not be reproduced, duplicated or transmitted without direct written permission from the author or the publisher.

Under no circumstances will any blame or legal responsibility be held against the publisher, or author, for any damages, reparation, or monetary loss due to the information contained within this book, either directly or indirectly.

Legal Notice:

This book is copyright protected. It is only for personal use. You cannot amend, distribute, sell, use, quote or paraphrase any part, or the content within this book, without the consent of the author or publisher.

Disclaimer Notice:

Please note the information contained within this document is for educational and entertainment purposes only. All effort has been executed to present accurate, up to date, reliable, complete information. No warranties of any kind are declared or implied. Readers acknowledge that the author is not engaged in the rendering of legal, financial, medical or professional advice. The content within this book has been derived from various sources. Please consult a licensed professional before attempting any techniques outlined in this book.

By reading this document, the reader agrees that under no circumstances is the author responsible for any losses, direct or indirect, that are incurred as a result of the use of the information contained within this document, including, but not limited to, errors, omissions, or inaccuracies.

Table of Contents

Introduction

"Confidence is not "I will profit on this trade." Confidence is "I will be fine if I don't profit from this trade." — Yvan Byeajee

How long have you been trading forex for? How long have you been successful at it? Forex trading is a fantastic way to make large sums of money, but the sad reality is that many traders who attempt this simply don't make it big. There are many reasons for this. Their mindsets are misaligned, perhaps their risk management is shoddy.

One of the biggest reasons, however, has to do with the strategies they choose to employ in the markets. Risk management and mindset are extremely important, but you can have the best risk management in the world and still fail. My point is that professional traders trade in a very specific manner and I'm going to show you how you too can trade this way in this book.

This is an advanced book for traders who have already mastered the basic skills I outlined in my previous book in this series. If you're already familiar with those, then you'll find that a lot of the concepts here build on those earlier ones. For those who are reading my books for the first time, welcome! If you happen to be an experienced trader who is looking to increase their profits, then you've come to the right place.

The markets can be as rewarding as they are frustrating and it often seems as if a very small percentage of traders happen to make the most money while the rest languish in mediocrity. I'm talking about making just enough money to break even or just enough money to earn a single-digit return per year.

You can use forex trading to greatly improve the quality of your life and that of your loved ones. It just comes down to how badly you want it.

Advanced Concepts

A lot of the concepts in this book will make you uncomfortable. What I mean is that I'll be presenting ways to trade that will strike you as being extremely counterintuitive. For example, I recommend that you trade price charts without any indicators whatsoever. I will show you how to do this in a step by step manner.

However, many traders are extremely uncomfortable with this since they're so used to receiving confirmation of an entry signal from an indicator. Accepting the fact that you don't need an indicator is going to be a tough pill to swallow. There are many such lessons in this book

In order to bring about changes in your results, you need to change the way you do things. You cannot play like a high school football player and expect to play in the NFL. It just isn't going to happen. In order to get to the pro level, you're going to have to change the way you do things and take them up a notch.

This is going to be uncomfortable and will challenge your comfort zone to an extreme level. Most people are not ready to make this leap. If you've picked up this book clearly you think that you need to make changes. Perhaps you aren't sure of the types of changes you need to make.

I'm here to show you exactly what you need to do. However, you're going to have to walk the path and as I said, it's going to require you to do things that will feel uncomfortable and counterintuitive. So, what are we talking about when it comes to advanced trading concepts? Is there some secret sauce that you've missed out on?

Yes and no. The fact is that the so-called secret is hidden in plain sight. Most traders miss out on it plainly because it doesn't seem complex enough. The method you will learn in this book upon which you will base all of your strategies is pretty simple to understand. However, trading it successfully is another thing entirely.

You will first need to refresh all of the basic knowledge you learned in the previous book and this is where you will begin. Following this, you're going to learn about the various elements that go into creating the market environment and the implications this has for your trading decisions.

Mindset and risk management play a very important role and in this book. We're going to dive a lot deeper into these topics compared to what you learned in the previous book. After all, if you're going to learn advanced techniques, you're going to have to master advanced risk management as well.

Throughout this book, I will be using language that assumes a certain degree of knowledge. For example, I'm not going to spend time discussing what a pip is or how you need to calculate an ideal position size (except for the first chapter where I'll recap the basics).

If you feel that these concepts are a bit out of your reach, I highly recommend studying the basics once again. At the very least, this book is ideal for traders who have been trading for a while and are looking to take that next step with their trading. You could be losing money or making money, it doesn't matter. As long as you have a decent amount of live trading experience, this book is for you.

Before we get into the basics of forex, allow me to properly introduce myself.

Who am I?

You know that my name is Edward Day seeing as you've bought my book. I am a full-time forex trader and I currently live in Chicago with my wife and two daughters. Economics and finance have always fascinated me since I was a kid and it was with this in mind that I studied finance and accounting in college.

A regular desk job followed graduation and despite having steady pay and a stable life, I knew I was destined for more. An accountant's job is essential I suppose but truth be told, it does get repetitive and boring after a while. I wanted to supplement my income in other ways and to also achieve a standard of living that would set me free.

I wanted to travel the world when I could and also enjoy a rich life. While my accounting desk job paid well, it also came with mind-numbing levels of boredom and an annoying boss who knew just enough to be the boss and didn't know enough to be supremely annoying.

It just so happened that one of my clients, who I would later become good friends with, was a full-time forex trader and his brokerage statements always fascinated me. I never did understand what all of those instrument tickers meant, and he invited me to a seminar he was attending.

Safe to say that I was hooked completely. The idea of speculating and being able to make money on a wide variety of geopolitical events fascinated me. It took me a while before I could make money in forex and a while longer before I could earn enough to quit my job. I can honestly say all of the struggles and heartbreak was worth it.

I've been trading full time since 2008 and these days I am a regular guest speaker on the seminar circuit here in Chicago and across America. I mentor students as well and my primary purpose in writing this book is to help people achieve their dreams.

Forex trading is a great way to do this and the markets are one of the few places these days that don't care about your qualifications or education. All that matters is whether you can do the work or not. For those who can, untold riches await. Those who can't eventually remove themselves from the game.

It doesn't matter what your current situation is. Whether you're so sick of your job that you want to take a ride out of there and never look back or if you're simply looking to make more money on the side, this book is your key to success. All I ask for in return is that you approach the knowledge contained in here with an open mind and that you give these methods the requisite amount of work they need.

They might not be the easiest of strategies, but I assure you they aren't complicated in any way. So, are you ready to change your trading and your life?

Let's move forward!

Chapter 1:

A Recap of the Basics

Before proceeding to look at the advanced material, it's best to review the basics once again. After all, if your basic knowledge isn't strong enough, there won't be much point in you trying to implement the methods in this book. Even if you feel that your knowledge is sound, I recommend that you read this chapter in detail.

This is because I will be referring to my previous book where I outlined a number of principles that will be expanded further here, especially when it comes to support and resistance and the way the market environment works. While reading the previous book in its entirety is ideal, this chapter is a brief summation of everything I spoke about there.

Let's begin by understanding what the market is.

FX Market Basics

People often think of the stock market when speaking of trading. The financial news rarely covers the FX market and you could be fooled into thinking that the stock market is the biggest and most important one out there. The truth is that the stock market is perhaps the smallest of all of them.

The bond and derivatives OTC markets dwarf the stock markets and influence them quite a lot. The FX market, in turn, dwarfs the bond market by many multiples. As of this writing, the average volume traded daily in the bond markets in the United States is close to $25 billion (Chen, 2020). The FX market comes in at $5.1 trillion per day.

One of the reasons for such huge volumes is that virtually every single major institution in the world is present in the FX markets. After all, FX deals with currencies and given the connection between a currency's strength and the overall economy it stands to reason that governments would actively take part in the markets.

Central banks all around the world are the mechanism through which governments exert force on the markets. While these actors are mostly concerned with maintaining the strength of their own respective currencies, they do have a massive impact on the flow of other currencies. For example, any policy decision on the Euro has an impact on related European currencies.

The first point of contrast between the stock and FX market is the timing or opening hours. While stock markets around the world are open for a few hours, usually eight or nine, per day the FX market is open 24/7. This provides the trader with a high degree of flexibility when it comes to choosing their times to trade.

The market officially begins or opens when Auckland comes online and as the day progresses, the rest of Asia comes online. This is commonly referred to as the Asian session. Typically, currencies of Oceania and Asia witness huge trading volumes at this time. Tokyo is the unofficial hub of the Asian session with the largest surge in volumes occurring at 8 A.M Tokyo time.

The great thing about FX is that being a global market, the trader can take advantage of overlaps. An overlap is when one market coincides with the opening of another, in a different part of the world. There are two significant overlaps when it comes to the FX market. The first occurs between the Asian markets and the opening of the European ones.

The first major European market to come online is Frankfurt, followed by Geneva and the rest of Western Europe. The last and most significant market to come online is London. Being one of the financial hubs of the world, trading volumes spike massively at 8 A.M London time and the first two hours of the London session coincides with the final two hours of the Asian session.

Overlaps such as these are great for traders because literally half the world is online at these times and liquidity and volatility spike. This means that the profit potential of trading in these times is significant. After all, volatility is the trader's friend when managed well.

As the Asian session comes to a close, the European session is in full swing. European currencies at this time receive significant boosts in volumes. As the day in Europe moves forward, the second overlap occurs. This overlap happens during the final four hours of the London session and the first four hours of the New York session.

Given that these two cities are the world's biggest financial centers, these four hours see a veritable explosion in trading volumes. Pretty much every currency finds high levels of liquidity and volatility here. There are many traders who choose to trade just this session solely thanks to this.

As London closes, a lot of the European currencies see a dip in volumes. New York carries the bulk of the session and at 5 P.M EST, the FX market hits an unofficial close. This is because once New York goes offline, there are no major trading volumes that emanate from the remaining centers that are open. While the market is open and there are small trades being placed, there is nothing of significance.

The market unofficially reopens once again at midnight New York time as Auckland comes back online and the Asian session once again begins. The 24-hour nature of the market offers great flexibility, but it comes with danger as well. The beginner trader is liable to think that they need to remain online throughout the entire market period and obviously, this is impossible.

There is also the danger of choosing the wrong session to trade or the wrong currency instrument to operate in given the session. For example, it hardly makes sense to trade the AUDJPY in the New York session.

While the trading hours of the FX market is very different from stock markets, the most significant difference is that the FX market is decentralized. Unlike the stock market which has a central order book, no such central exchange exists in FX. The entire market is a network of bank dealers. Thus, without the central order book, there is zero possibility of front running which a few high-frequency trading firms take advantage of.

This doesn't mean there is zero algorithmic presence in FX. Far from it. However, you are unlikely to pay an additional point every time you place a trade thanks to front running HFT firms not being present.

FX instruments are a different breed in their own right. Let's take a look at how these work.

Instruments

FX instruments are currency pairs and these pairs reflect the exchange rate that is prevalent at the time. For example, if the EURUSD is selling for 1.3245, this can be read as One Euro is equivalent to 1.3245 USD. The first currency in the pair is called the base currency and the second is referred to as the quote currency.

While stock and bond prices move in USD or any equivalent currency, the same is not true of FX pairs. After all, they have two currencies built within them so there is some translation needed. The smallest unit of movement within an FX pair is called a pip. A pip is equivalent to 0.0001. Therefore, from our previous example, if the price of EURUSD moved from 1.3245 to 1.3247, the price has moved by two pips.

The only exception to this is the JPY denominated pairs where a pip is equivalent to 0.01. Calculating the value of a single pip in your equivalent currency can get complicated and for this reason, it is best to use an online position size calculator. You will find an excellent one at **https://www.babypips.com/tools/position-size-calculator**.

Forex brokers typically provide another type of instrument called a contract for difference or CFD. CFDs are instruments that mimic the movement of other financial instruments. Thus, they are derivatives. For example, many brokers offer a CFD titled USOil. This CFD mimics the movement of the WTI contracts on the NYMEX. Similarly, there are CFDs derived from the FTSE 100, the Dow Jones and S&P 500 and so on. CFDs are a great way to gain exposure to foreign markets but the downside is that you are at the mercy of your broker in terms of liquidity.

After all, these contracts are issued by your broker and are specific to them. It is your broker who takes the other side of your CFD trade, for the most part. In case your broker doesn't have a dealing desk, the orders are distributed amongst other traders who are trading with the broker. Thus, liquidity can be an issue at times. However, as long as your position size is small, you're unlikely to have any issues.

Some brokers also offer options on FX pairs along with binary options. I didn't cover binary options in my previous book simply because they're such a magnificently terrible proposition for traders that it's not worth spending any time discussing them. As far as regular options go, you can trade them as regular instruments or use options trading strategies to profit from them.

Perhaps the most significant thing a broker offers in FX is leverage and understanding this is crucial to your success.

Leverage

Since FX instruments move in units of 0.0001, the probability of making a profit without leverage is close to zero. What I mean is that they just don't move very much in terms of dollars and cents. The average price movement of the EURUSD pair over the course of 24 hours is probably 100 pips. This is around one cent per day.

It stands to reason that FX pairs move very little. After all, you don't see exchange rates fluctuating by too much, do you? If this happened entire economies would collapse. For example, if you took off from New York when the Euro was worth a dollar and a half and landed in Paris to find that the rate had doubled, you can be certain that there's going to be economic chaos.

This is why traders need leverage to magnify their gains. In the United States, FX brokers can offer leverage up to 1:50. This means for every dollar you place as margin, you can borrow $50 from the broker. Internationally, brokers offer as much as 1:500. Leverage isn't necessarily a good thing despite being necessary.

You want to have a decent amount of it but too much of it will erase your gains and cause you losses that are well in excess of your original investment amount. Your broker will require you to maintain a certain amount of margin in your account at all times and if your account balance happens to fall below this level, you will be issued a margin call.

A margin call is a notice from your broker instructing you to deposit more money into your account. Failing this, the broker will exit whatever positions you have in the market and will recover anything that they can. FX brokers are a different breed from their stock market counterparts.

This is especially true internationally. Within the US the most significant piece of legislation you should be aware of is that the PDT rule does not apply to FX markets (Chen, 2020). Thus, if you happen to have low levels of capital to trade with, the FX markets are a great way to begin.

While this doesn't occur in the U.S, the practice of 'B' booking happens quite a lot in forex. This is just another way of saying that the broker buckets their customers' orders and trades against them. Generally speaking, B booking happens to those traders who have low account balances and who have losing records after a month or so in their accounts.

FX brokers can also earn money by charging a markup on the price spread before filling your trade. These kinds of brokers offer zero commission accounts and many newbie traders willingly open such accounts thanks to marketing working its magic. However, the fact is that this ultimately costs the trader a few points per trade and this adds up to significant amounts over time.

The best FX brokers to open an account with are straight-through processing brokers (STP) who pass their customers' orders directly to their liquidity providers. STP brokers may also be tagged as being so-called Electronic Communication Network (ECN) brokers. While there are small differences in the way in which STP and ECNs operate, you won't go wrong with either type.

Lots

When placing trades in stocks you will buy shares. With FX, you buy lots. A standard lot is 100,000 units of the quote currency, with 10,000 called a mini lot and 1,000 called a micro lot. There are so-called nano lots of 100 as well but not many brokers offer these.

Brokers can quote the order quantity in two ways. They can either specify the entire quantity (121,000) or in an abbreviated fashion (1.21). In order to calculate your ideal position size according to your risk limits, use the position size calculator previously highlighted.

Order Types

Successful traders understand the different types of orders that are available at their disposal and use them accordingly. Market orders will result in order fills at prevailing market prices no matter how bad that might be for your profitability. If the price of the instrument spikes right when you decide to enter into a position, you will receive that inflated price.

To mitigate this risk, brokers have what is called a limit order. A limit order comes with a trigger built into it. As long as the market price is in a position above or below this limit, whichever is better for your trade's profitability, your order will be executed. Once the market price moves into a position that is detrimental to your entry, your broker will not execute the order.

For example, if you've shorted the EURUSD at 1.3245 and have placed this price as the trigger, your broker will execute this order as long as the market price is equal to or greater than this price. This is because if the market price declines below this, your profit on your short position will decrease. You want prices to be as high as possible when shorting since this is what will enable you to make a bigger profit.

The downside of limit orders is that you'll sometimes find that your order hasn't been filled completely. If the market price moves past the trigger before the entire order has been filled, you'll be stuck with a partial fill. To get past this particular deficiency, brokers provide stop orders.

A stop order places a premium on the order being fully filled no matter what the price is. There is a trigger but once the trigger is hit, the entire order is executed no matter what. This is particularly useful when traders are looking to exit losing trades. In such scenarios, traders seek to exit no matter what and limit orders don't quite cut it in such scenarios.

Stop orders are also useful when traders seek to enter once a price action signal has been thrown. For example, if you spot a bullish candlestick price pattern and want to enter once the price moves past the higher of that bar, a buy stop order does the job nicely. A limit order is more suited for situations when you wish to enter before the price has hit a level or reached it.

In the previous book, I suggested the use of stop and market orders as being the most useful ones given the strategies that were highlighted in there. In this book, you will find that limit orders, combined with stop orders for stop losses will be far more applicable.

Candlesticks

One of the best ways to represent price movements on a chart is via candlesticks. Originally invented by a Japanese rice trade back in the 1600s, candlesticks have long since moved past their original Japanese origins. There are many different patterns but instead of memorizing all of their names and shapes, the best way to analyze them is to look at the underlying order flow that produces those shapes.

The first pattern that you should be aware of is the pin bar. Pin bars have small bodies and comparatively large tails or wicks. A pin with a long wick is a bearish signal while one with a long tail is a bullish signal. The best way to enter these signals is by placing the stop loss order either above or below the candle and entering on the close of the bar or once price has moved past the high of the bar.

The best pins are found near support or resistance levels. Another thing to keep in mind is that pins are best used as continuation patterns. In other words, look for them to form in small sideways movements within a trend or within the trending portion itself and use them to enter trends.

A lot of traders try to use pins as reversal patterns but trend reversals are far more complex phenomena than a single pin can indicate. What I mean is that despite the pin being the one we pay attention to and use as a signal, it doesn't make sense to ignore all of the other bars that exist on the chart. Just because they don't have a recognizable shape doesn't mean they're irrelevant.

The second pattern to pay attention to is the two bar reversal. This is a two-bar pattern with the second bar being the exact opposite of the first. A bearish bar followed by a bullish one is a bullish signal while a bullish bar followed by a bearish one is a bearish signal. The idea behind the pattern is that when both bars are superimposed upon one another, they form a pin bar.

Just like the pin bar, you want to look for these near support or resistance levels. In addition to this, they are best used as continuation patterns like the pin bar is used. The size of the two bars relative to the bars that surround them is important with larger bars providing better quality signals.

The third candlestick pattern to pay attention to is the outside bar. These are pretty easy to spot due to the fact that they're pretty huge in size and tend to dominate the chart whenever they form. Unlike the other two patterns, these are a reversal pattern and you should look for these at the end of a trend. The direction of the outside bar dictates the direction you want to enter in.

What I mean is that if the outside bar happens to be bearish, you want to enter short. These bars usually form near strong support and resistance levels and often mark the beginning of the period where trends begin to reverse.

Trends do not reverse over the course of a few bars and in fact, this process takes a long time. However, outside bars are a great way to find the beginning of these phases and you'll be able to position yourself accordingly.

When trading these price patterns remember to look at the underlying order flow dynamics instead of simply trying to spot the perfect shapes. This will help you drift through those instances where the shape of the bar will be right but the underlying conditions will be a mismatch. For example, don't try to enter a bullish pin bar in a bearish trend.

The shape might be right but the conditions are completely wrong and therefore, this is not a valid signal. Always pay attention to order flow. You're going to learn a lot more about order flow in this book and once you figure this out, you won't need patterns to signal entries.

Support and Resistance

You can have all the price patterns in the world on your side but if you don't ally them with support and resistance levels, your trades are unlikely to succeed. This is because support and resistance levels are created by traders expressing their opinions about the prices in the market.

Trading success is all about positioning yourself in the path of least resistance. What this means is that you should seek to align yourself with the crowd as much as possible. Contrarianism is not a very successful strategy in the markets and it cannot be pulled off by everyone who practices it. Therefore, seek to identify the signs that indicate that traders are positioning themselves at certain spots in the market and place your orders accordingly.

Support and resistance levels offer the best indications of these spots. Price repeatedly interacts with these levels and this affirms the fact that there are traders present at those levels that are willing to defend it. Broadly speaking, there are three kinds of support and resistance levels you should be aware of.

The first is swing points. The force with which price moves into the swing point and the relative force and angle with which price leaves it are indicative of how strong the level is. The size of the bars that leave the level also indicates the strength of the traders present at the level. Bigger bars are indicative of greater trader strength and if the price happens to retest the level at a later point, placing a limit order at that point in anticipation of a bounce is a good move.

The second type of level you should watch out for are places from which price has had strong reactions in the past. These can be swing points or it could be a range boundary. Often such levels will change their character and will begin to behave in the opposite manner once they're broken. What I mean is that a strong support level that is broken will often act as resistance and a broken resistance will act as support.

The greater the number of times that a level has been tested, the stronger it is. Once price breaks past, you can safely place a trade in the opposite direction and enter in the direction of the new movement. The third kind of support and resistance level you should be aware of is dynamic resistance levels.

Moving average lines are the best type of dynamic resistance there are and the most commonly used one is the 20 EMA. This is because a lot of professional traders tend to use this indicator. While they use it for a variety of reasons, when trends are strong, you will find that prices will bounce off this line quite a lot and you can safely enter.

The price environment is pretty important when it comes to using dynamic support and resistance. They typically work only when the trend is strong. The best way to determine this is to look at the angle at which prices are progressing. If you see prices declining or rising at a steep angle, this means that the trend is strong.

Another type of support and resistance level you should watch out for is one that exists prominently on the higher time frame as well. For example, if you're trading the H4 and you see that an upcoming level exists on the D1 and W1, odds are good that price is going to react strongly at this level.

The thing to keep in mind about support and resistance is that they are zones. Many traders draw horizontal lines to represent them and fall into the mistake of thinking that these lines accurately represent levels. The fact is that support and resistance is created by traders and traders exist on multiple time frames.

Traders on different time frames will place their orders at varying distances. Thus, you will rarely see a perfectly horizontal level. Instead, a cluster is more likely and this is what gives rise to zones. Traders operating on higher time frames will place their orders in the shallow portion of the zone while those operating in lower time frames will place them deep in the zone.

Indicators

Technical indicators are used extensively by traders and for good reason. They do a lot to illuminate the state of order flow in the market. There are a large number of them present these days and it can be tough to decide which ones to use. The problem with indicators is that the way in which they ought to be used changes over time.

This happens because the markets change their nature and as more traders use indicators in a certain way, that indicator becomes less reliable. Therefore, the best way to implement indicators in a trading strategy is to look at some evergreen ways of using them and to use them in the right conditions.

The first indicator that helps with this is the ADX. The ADX has different components to it but the most important one to pay attention to is the ADX line itself. As long as its value is over 25, this indicates the presence of a trend. The greater the value of the ADX line, the stronger the trend is.

The ADX is a great indicator for traders to use because of its simplicity and the fact that the information it provides is invaluable. By knowing the strength of the trend at all times, traders can align themselves with the market accordingly and utilize appropriate strategies.

Given the way in which it is used, the ADX can also be combined with other indicators to produce trading systems that work under all market conditions. One of the indicators that it can be combined with is the RSI or Relative Strength Index. The RSI is an oscillator and its values are bound between zero and 100. The RSI window is divided into a neutral zone, an oversold one and an overbought one.

The idea is that when the indicator moves into the overbought zone, bears will enter the market and push prices back down to restore equilibrium. When prices move into the oversold zone, bulls step in and push prices back up. The catch is that the RSI should be used only in sideways moving or ranging markets.

Using the RSI in a trend will lead to losses since, in a trend, the RSI will hang around in the extreme zones for long periods of time. In combination with the ADX, the RSI works wonders. Use the RSI when the ADX indicates that there is a weak trend or no trend on and you can implement it in the right conditions.

The third indicator that you can use is the parabolic stop and reverse or SAR. The SAR prints as a series of dots on the price chart and these can be above or below prices. If they happen to be above, this is a bearish signal while dots below price are bullish. The time to enter long or short is when the dots flip their positions.

The SAR is a trading system all by itself and it works very well in trending environments and will keep you in your trades for a while. In ranging environments, it works really well since the price ranges tend to be large. The only environment in which it will throw false signals is when markets move in small sideways patterns.

These usually happen in between trending movies and trading these can be frustrating. You'll likely find that the SAR will have you entering and exiting at a high rate. Despite this, the thing to keep in mind is that over the long term, the SAR will make you a lot of money as long as you stick with it and follow its signals.

Bollinger bands are another neatly packaged trading system within an indicator. There are two ways of using it and you can use either one of them or use both to form a third trading system. The first way to use it is to watch out for bounces off the centerline (20 EMA) in strong trends. This is pretty much the same as trading the dynamic support and resistance that the 20 EMA creates.

The second method is to use the outer envelopes as regions where you can watch for price bounces and place a trade in the direction of the bounce. Keep in mind that you should use this method of trading only in ranges. Thus, when you combine the two methods, you have a system that is suited for all sorts of market scenarios.

There are far more complex indicators than these, some of which even employ differential calculus to arrive at conclusions, but in the market, complexity rarely rewards you. The best way to trade is to keep it simple. Besides, technical inputs and entry signals are just one half of successful trading.

The other half is risk management

Managing Risk

Many traders ignore the risk management part of trading and think that as long as they have great entry signals, they'll be fine. The thing with trading is that it isn't an orderly system like the exams you used to take in school. In an exam, the greater number of questions you answer correctly, the higher your score is and the more successful you are.

When it comes to trading, the number of times you're correct is immaterial. What matters is the combination of how many times you're correct (your win rate) and the extent to which you're correct compared to when you're incorrect (your reward to risk ratio).

Both of these combine together to produce a profitability equation that you must always keep in mind when trading. This means that your risk per trade needs to be consistent and it should be a fixed percentage of your account. Your exits should always be at a level that is above your breakeven reward to risk ratio levels.

I'm not going to dive into the math behind these two numbers since I'm assuming that as an experienced trader you will know these well. If you do have any doubts about this, please refer to my previous book on this topic. For now, let's move on and look at another risk factor that many traders ignore.

This is their risk of ruin. The risk of ruin defines the probability of losing all of your capital. As long as this is maintained at zero, your capital will always be safe and by definition, you will make money. To ensure your risk of ruin is zero you will need to reduce your per-trade risk and this causes a lot of problems for traders.

They feel that by risking small amounts, there's no way they'll ever make big money. Well, it is possible to make large sums of money in the markets, but it isn't by doing things irrationally. As long as you maintain good risk management, money and capital will find you and you will be able to earn millions.

The wrong way to do it is to risk an undue sum of money in the hopes that you can earn outsized returns of 100% or 200% or some such nonsensical value. Keep your risk low and consistent and you'll end up attracting capital and investment to you.

A trading journal is of paramount importance when it comes to risk management. This is because you can not down both the information surrounding the trade as well as your mental state when you entered or exited the trade. Reviewing this journal at the end of every week is extremely important and you should make it a part of your routine.

Speaking of routines, many traders do not prepare well for the markets. They think that they'll be able to trade well despite staying up all night and not sleeping well. This belief comes about due to the fact that they think that trading success is all about following an entry signal and that's it.

As you've probably experienced, this is hardly how it works. Keeping the money you've made is a tough task and in order to do this, you need to practice sound risk management techniques. Maintain an established routine and prepare for the markets in all seriousness.

Take some time to practice your skills and always prioritize your mental well being over your need to trade. At the end of the day, your brain is your biggest asset and if you feel the need to trade despite feeling low or harassed, you're in a poor mental state and are guaranteed to lose money in the market.

Scaling

The most important part of your trading plan is to determine how you will scale into your trading business. The way to do this is to follow three simple steps. Your first step should be to purchase a simulation software that will allow you to replay historical market bars. Practice your skills in this environment and once you've learned them well and developed your strategy, place simulated trades.

Aim to place at least 1,000 trades with the aim of capturing relevant statistical data. This is where you will find the average win to loss ratio of your system as well as your win rate. See if these make you money. Only when you've done this over 1,000 trades should you move to the next step.

The next step is to open a demo account with your broker. Many forex brokers provide demo accounts for free, so you won't have any problems finding one. Place your demo trades as if you're trading the market with live money and aim to make money over the course of six consecutive months.

It doesn't need to be big money but once this is done, you can begin trading live. Take it easy and start off with just a couple of instruments. Expand your portfolio by utilizing the same scaling technique as you did for your first two instruments. Over time you'll find that your portfolio size increases, and you'll make more money (Hall, 2020).

There are ways to make millions of course. I'll discuss these at the end of this book. For now, simply focus on trading according to proper risk management principles and master the technical skills of your trading system.

Chapter 2:

The Anatomy of Ranges

Now that we've reviewed the basics, it's time to get into the good stuff. This chapter deals with ranges and the next one will deal with trends. Ranges and trends are the two basic movements that the market makes and in order to make money, you need to understand them thoroughly.

Keep in mind that the systems I'm about to show you are extremely discretionary. They do not involve the use of indicators. Thus, your mental state is of paramount importance as is the amount of work you're willing to put into learning this material. These methods are not found in mainstream trading advice, but I assure you that this is how professional traders evaluate the market.

Professional traders at banks or in proprietary trading firms do not rely on indicators to help them decide when to enter markets. Instead, they look at order flow. Over the next two chapters, this is what we're trying to do: Develop a system to analyze order flow.

Sideways Moves

A range is a sideways movement in the market. Perhaps a better way to think of it is that it is a non-directional move. Having said that do not expect a range to be a perfect horizontal movement. You will often find ranges that have a small directional bias to them. What is important is that you understand why we classify them as ranges in the first place.

There are two kinds of ranges you will find in the market. The first is the type of range that exists within trends. The second is the range that occurs at the end of a trend. Both of these types of ranges have very different orders of mechanisms going on within them. In order to understand them better, we need to take a step back and first understand where orders come from.

How Order Flow is Created

Order flow simply refers to the buy and sell orders that trades are currently placing in the market for an instrument. Simple enough, isn't it? At any given moment in time, there are millions of orders in the market and we have no way of knowing who is placing how much and in what direction they are trading.

Unlike the stock market, there is no Level II access in FX. Even if there was, it doesn't help much because of the decentralized nature of the market. You'll never receive a full snapshot of everything that is going on. A great way of evaluating order flow is to look at trade volumes.

Unfortunately, the decentralized nature of the market negates this as well. Your broker will know the volumes local to their LP and perhaps the LPs who are on either side of their network. This is hardly enough to capture the entire volume of orders. Hence, we're left with only one resource: The price chart itself.

Why should we bother to even analyze order flow? After all, can't we just use indicators and patterns? Order flow is what gives indicators their meaning and it is what creates price action patterns in the first place. Would you rather use a signal that is derived from something or use the source of the signal itself?

By deciphering order flow you'll be able to obtain better entries for your trades since you'll be a step ahead of the rest of the traders who use indicators and have to wait for confirmation from them. Remember that all indicators are lagging ones despite their creators claiming otherwise. After all, every indicator is built on the back of price action. If no price action exists, how can the indicator possibly predict the future? The thought is preposterous.

Therefore, the best thing to do is to evaluate order flow and determine the path of least resistance using it.

Trends and ranges are manifestations of order flow in the markets and they occur due to the way in which it is balanced. The entire sum of order flow in the market can be divided into bullish versus bearish orders. At any point in time, there is a proportion that exists (Keupper, 2020).

We can use trends and ranges to figure out this proportion and align ourselves with the dominant force accordingly. Ranges are primarily caused by balanced order flow. When the proportion of bulls and bears is equal in the market, you will see prices moving sideways.

This makes intuitive sense. Think of it in terms of opposite forces being exerted on a piece of wood. If both forces are equal, the piece of wood isn't going anywhere. The minute one force overpowers the other, even to a small extent, the piece will move in the direction of the force.

Thus, whenever you see a range, keep in mind that both sides of the market are currently balanced and this is why prices are nondirectional. Keep in mind that both sides are balanced for now. This state of affairs will not last forever. This is why we need to differentiate between the two types of ranges that are formed.

Depending on the type of range present in the market, we can determine the likely path of price once the range ends.

Ranges in a Trend

The first type of range we will look at is one that is formed in the middle of a trend. Despite moving in a particular direction, prices rarely do so in a sustained manner. Trends take many breaks in between and it is the nature of these breaks in directional movement that we receive clues as to which way price might be headed next.

A common fear of all traders is to ask themselves how they can possibly know when a trend is coming to an end. In other words, they wish to trade with the trend but how long should they remain in the trade? What if price goes the other way shortly? Analyzing the type of ranges formed gives us the best clues as to all of this.

Let's begin by looking at the ranges present in Figure 1.

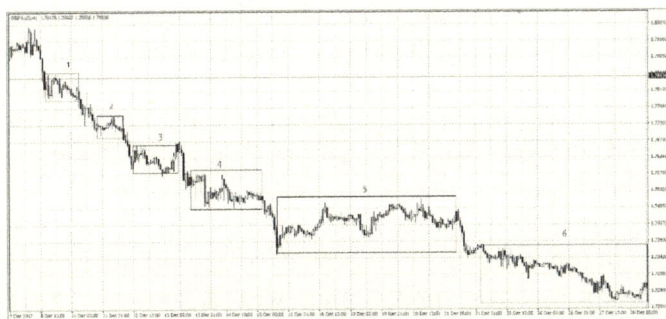

Figure 1: GBPAUD H1 Downtrend

Figure 1 shows the GBPAUD pair in a long downtrend on the H1 timeframe. The different ranges that occur are indicated by boxes labeled 1 through 6. The first step to take here is to simply get a feel for the manner in which the ranges are changing as the trend progresses.

At the beginning of this trend, order flow is heavily tilted towards the bearish side. Price drops without much pushback from the bears and it takes a breather. This results in the small sideways movement that occurs at box 1. Notice how small this box is. It isn't important for you to mark the exact moment or bar at which the range begins or ends. As long as you mark the gist of it, this is fine.

Such small ranges typically occur in the beginning of trends. They're forming not because of a balanced order flow between both sides of the market but more because the bears withdraw for a short period and the bulls don't have much in the way of representation.

Going back to our previous example of the plank of wood. Imagine that it is being pushed in one direction strongly and then that force diminishes. Due to the fact that there is very little or no opposing force, this withdrawal will cause the piece of wood to remain where it is. This is pretty much what is happening here with box 1. The bears are taking a breather and the bulls are non-existent.

Price soon continues moving downwards once again. Box 2 indicates a range that barely exists for a few bars and this is about as big as box 1 is. This indicates that the bulls are still dormant and haven't found much of a footing against the bears. Prices continue to decline and then we come to box 3.

Box 3 starts off much in the same way as the previous two ones but notice the manner in which it finishes. There is a strong bullish push. Not only is it strong, but it also lasts for three consecutive bars without the bears doing anything to stop it. It eventually hits the closest resistance and price continues to fall down once more.

Despite this, box 3 is a significant one. Notice that this is the largest box we've had in a while and this is also the first time the bulls have put up any sort of resistance to the downward pressure in the market. This indicates that they're finding their feet even if they're not in a position to challenge the bears completely yet.

With this in mind, we should be on the lookout for longer ranges since clearly, we can expect the bulls to grow stronger. This happens just as we expected at box 4. This is even bigger in length than the previous one and you can see how the bulls manage to hold prices at this level for quite a while. There is an initial strong bearish push, but this dissipates and price simply floats at this level for a while.

Price declines some more and we soon find ourselves in box 5. This is by far the largest range in terms of size and it represents some pretty balanced price action within it. Not only is it the longest it is also the largest in terms of height. This indicates that price is swinging back and forth within it thanks to the bulls and bears pushing prices up and down.

Previously, the bears had been withdrawing to a large extent within ranges but now we can see that this is not the case. They're actively appearing within the range in order to push bulls back down. This can only mean that they're recognizing greater bullish strength and need to appear in greater numbers to contain it.

At this point it pays to take stock of everything that we've observed. We've seen that bullish presence is gradually increasing as time goes on and the bears are facing increasingly stiff competition. While they still have the upper hand, clearly, they don't have a large majority in terms of the order flow proportion.

You can choose to give these proportions numbers if you like, if that helps you understand what's happening better. For example, you could say that the current order flow is split 60/40 in favor of the bears and so on. Whatever you do, as long as you're building a picture of which way the market is headed, you'll be fine.

Given the increasing bullish presence, we need to start looking out for the end of the trend. At this point, we don't know when this will occur. All we know is that if the bullish presence keeps increasing, soon the proportion will reach 50/50 and then eventually, it's going to go the other way in favor of the bulls.

Getting back to our chart, we see that price falls some more and then goes into an off downward movement. This is marked by box 6. I have marked it as such because this is also a sideways movement even if the direction of price isn't sideways. Why is this? It all has to do with the way price is behaving.

If this were a true trending movement, you would expect prices to move a lot faster in the downward direction. Instead, look at the distribution of the bars within this box. There's an equal number of bullish and bearish bars within it. This means that in this region, both bulls and bears hold equal sway.

Another point to notice is the size of the bars here. They're pretty small and are equivalent to the size of bars within the previous ranges, on average. All of this indicates that after the initial bearish push down, both sides of the market are engaged in a tussle once again and this time, going by the distribution of bars alone, we can see that they're far more balanced.

As we reach the right edge of this chart, what conclusions can we draw? How should we trade this chart as it stands?

For one thing, we can clearly see that we're moving into a range or are already in the initial portions of a big one. We can expect price swings in both directions. This is because the ranges have been getting bigger until now and the previous one saw decent price swings. This means the swings in this range are going to be even greater.

We also know that if this range happens to be a particularly large one, we can expect the trend to end and for prices to begin moving in the other direction. Again, we can't predict the exact moment when this will happen, but we know we're close to it. The price might decline some more, and it might move in bigger ranges. All of this brings us closer to the end of the bear trend and we need to keep this in mind.

We'll pick up what happens in the next section but for now, let's take the time to look at some of the attributes of the ranges we've seen thus far. As you can see, they're formed due to two reasons. Earlier in the trend, they formed because the bears simply withdrew. This created small ranges where price didn't really push back against the trend and simply went perfectly sideways.

Sometimes, you might see ranges that move slightly in the direction of the trend with very small bearish bars. The same thing is happening within these ranges as well. The bears have withdrawn and the bulls are non-existent (the opposite is the case in a bullish trend obviously. The bulls withdraw and the bears are non-existent and the range moves slightly upwards). As time goes on and as bullish participation increases, the ranges grow in size and height.

The increase in height is a reflection of the fact that price is swinging in both directions. It is pushing back into the trend to a greater degree and this is causing the bears to enter and push prices back down to reassert the trend. Another indicator of this increasing bearish participation is the distribution of the bars within the boxes.

As time goes on, we see a more balanced distribution. As the boxes get bigger, the proportion of bullish to bearish bars becomes increasingly balanced. In the earlier ranges, you might see a large number of bullish bars but given how small they are, this is hardly an indicator of bulls entering.

A point I would like to make here is that you should not develop rigid rules regarding the size of boxes and so on. Don't create a rule to the effect of 'if a box is large it means order flow is balanced' and so on. You need to develop the picture by looking at what happened previously.

The number of bullish bars in the earlier, small ranges do not bother us because we know we're at the beginning of a trend. The size of the range supports this observation and we draw a conclusion. We don't draw the conclusion on the basis of the size of the box alone.

Now we find ourselves in a situation where price seems to be declining but it isn't doing it with much gusto. Given what has transpired before, with the bulls increasing their presence in the market, it is reasonable to expect a big sideways movement in both length and height.

Let's move forward in time and see what happens.

Ranges at the End of a Trend

Figure 2 is an illustration of what takes place after the edge of Figure 1.

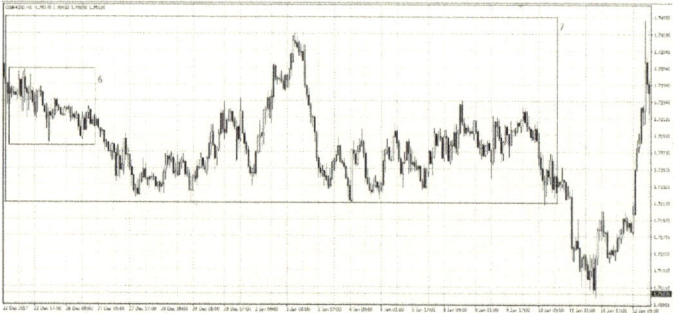

Figure 2: GBPAUD Continued

In Figure 2 you can see the box 6 marked and this is where we left off from Figure 1. However, as the picture develops fully, we can see that 6 is really just a part of a bigger box labeled 7. Notice how the price movement is sideways despite prices gyrating up and down. Also notice how huge this range is in terms of length as well as height. There is a peak in between and a subsequent decline that marks the greatest point of bullish versus bearish struggle.

Starting from the left, we were correct in assuming that the anemic downswing in the trend was partly because the bulls and bears both withdrew from the market. As price reaches the bottom of box 7, the bulls spring into action and create what is easily the largest pushback in the entire trend. Look back at Figure 1 and you'll see that the bulls have not managed to push this far back ever nor in such a sustained manner.

As prices rise, there are no bears to be found. Eventually, bearish pressure returns and prices are slammed right back down and this creates a V shape. Despite this, the bulls manage to hold the support at the bottom of box 7. Eventually, after a lot of struggle with the bulls, the bears break this support level.

By this point, though there are some clear conclusions we can draw with regards to the state of the downtrend. We've just had a huge range where the bulls showed some serious strength. They pushed prices up and managed to hold a support level despite the bears slamming into it. This means that the bulls are at least as strong as the bears, if not stronger.

All of this should put us on alert for a change in the trend. Perhaps this range will prove itself to be the range that occurs at the end of a trend. Given that price has just nosedive once again we don't know for sure as yet. As such, we're still bearish but clearly there is serious bullish strength that could potentially turn the trend the other way.

This turn comes soon enough. Notice how forcefully prices rise back up. This is about as clear an upswing as you'll ever see. However, as we reach the edge of Figure 2, we're still holding our slightly bearish bias despite this upward push. At this point, prices have not cleared the top of the previous peak in range 7.

Remember that this is where the bears pushed back the strongest bullish challenge. As such, this is a pretty important resistance level. In this time frame, as long as that resistance level holds, we cannot claim with any certainty that the bears have been extinguished.

There is an important lesson here: Despite the order flow balance clearly tilting towards a balanced one (or slightly in favor of the bulls) we don't immediately flip our bias. This is because our aim here isn't to call the exact moment when the trend flips. Instead, we need to wait and see what the crowd is doing.

As of this moment, as the right edge of Figure 3 proves, there is significant bearish presence at that resistance level. Notice the wick on the huge bullish bar. The bears are still strong enough to resist a move of that size. By 'move' I'm not talking about the single bar that hits the resistance.

I'm talking of the entire chain that rises from the lows to this level. It's just one huge bullish move. Despite this, in a 50/50 environment, the bears are strong enough to push back. This means that the crowd is not fully in favor of turning bullish as yet. This level is the line in the sand and when this breaks, that is when we switch our bias and turn bullish.

If prices turn back down after this, we simply extend the range boundaries of box 7 horizontally. If prices break past this level, box 7 will have been the range at the end of a trend. Notice that you don't need to make this distinction in real-time. What you instead need to be doing is reading how the price is behaving within the range and relate it to what has happened before it.

Noticing the force with which price collides against support or resistance levels and drawing conclusions about the relative order flow distribution is what matters. As such, assuming that this is the range at the end of a trend, notice that it is easily the largest in all terms.

The price bars are almost evenly distributed between bullish and bearish and the price action within the range is quite volatile. As such, the best places to trade these ranges from are at the boundaries. These large ranges also call for a different trading approach than the ones you saw before.

In the earlier ranges, the order flow was clearly tilted towards the bearish side. Here, we've seen that this isn't the case. The bulls are just as strong as the bears and are asserting themselves pretty well. This means you can trade both long and short within these ranges. You're likely to find enough of a crowd to push prices your way no matter which side you trade.

As I already mentioned the best locations from which to place your trade is the upper or lower boundaries of the range. In the case of the previous ranges, your best bet is to trade the upper boundaries and enter short in the direction of the trend. If the trend was bullish, you would enter at the range support.

Trade Entries and Stop Losses

You might be wondering what I mean when I say 'enter'. Don't you need a signal or some indicator to do so? Not really. You know the price environment, you know the direction in which price is headed. What more confirmation do you need? You simply place a limit order at the top of the range and place your stop loss above the range resistance. Once price hits your limit, you're in a trade.

The same applies for when you want to go long. Place your limit on the support and stop-loss some distance away. Wait for the price to hit your limit (or enter at market when it reaches there) and enter your trade. Simple.

Your reward can be placed at either your chosen profit multiple (reward to risk ratio) or you can ride the price all the way till the trend ends. You'll learn how to spot these points in the next chapter. If you're entering a counter-trend trade in a large end of trend type range, you can ride prices back to the other boundary.

Trading in this manner will seem odd to you at first and you're going to feel uncomfortable. You're not waiting for any indicator or anything of the sort. You're simply reading the ranges and trading them as such. This is how professionals trade and it is in your best interest to trade this way.

For now, let's get back to the GBPAUD and see what happens next.

Conclusion

Figure 3: GBPAUD Range Break

Figure 3 shows that once the price tested the all-important resistance level at the top, it hung around there in a smaller sideways movement for a while. Notice that this range is just a part of the overall larger range that was marked by Box 7. We simply extend its horizontal boundary to include all of this.

Also notice that price seems very reluctant to drop downwards. It keeps hanging around the resistance level and eventually tests it again as the chart ends. Given everything that has happened, what can we conclude is most likely going to happen here?

Clearly bullish strength has been increasing. The bears have been holding this level pretty well for a while, but they seem to be unable to push prices down much below this level. Notice the positions of the rectangle on the left and the one on the right in Figure 3. See how the one on the right is much higher?

This clearly shows that prices are making higher lows which is a clear indication of increasing bullish pressure. As price prepares to break out of this range, we can either trade the breakout using a stop order with a trigger on the other side of the resistance or we can wait for a retest since this is a strong resistance level being broken. Remember that if the price doesn't run away from the level after breaking out, it will likely retest it as support and then move higher.

Trading the breakout is a risky move but you're far more likely to be in the trade. The problem is that if the breakout fails, you're going to eat a loss. Waiting for the retest is also risky because you're likely to miss out on the breakout if it is a strong one. However, it is the safer play.

Your choice comes down to what type of trader you want to be. An aggressive trader will go for the breakout. A conservative one will wait for the retest. Both ways are correct and perfectly profitable. The best way to test this would be to simulate it as a part of your scaling plan and see what works for you.

As you can see, we've just traded an entire downtrend and its end using just the ranges that were present within it. We haven't even looked at the support and resistance characteristics or even the quality of the trend. You can be very successful trying to enter using ranges and simply trading their boundaries.

However, understanding the mechanics of the trending portions will turbocharge your results. Before you move on, take the time to analyze a few charts of your own and pay special attention to the types of ranges you see. Don't worry initially about how you would trade them.

Just classify them as being small ranges at the beginning of a trend or the end of trend ranges. From there, see how you would enter them. Don't place any mental trades, just earmark the spots where you could likely enter and leave it at that. Profit and loss can come later.

Chapter 3:

The Anatomy of Trends

It sounds odd to say this, but trends are comprised of both trending and range parts. You've already seen how ranges occur within a trend and how this can be used to predict the direction of the trend and how much longer it has to run. In this chapter, we're going to pay more attention to the trending portions and see what we can learn from them.

The good news is that range analysis does a lot of the heavy lifting when it comes to this method, so you don't need to worry too much if you get the trend portions wrong.

Why Trends Occur

The first topic to address is to answer why trends even occur in the first place. What possesses prices to move in this direction and then that? The simple answer is supply and demand. I mentioned the bulls and the bears in the previous chapter and the truth is that these are pretty broad umbrellas within which I'm classifying market participants.

There are all kinds of traders in the market and they have different motivations. A central bank might be selling AUD and buying GBP in order to reduce its exposure to that currency and it might be trying to buy more USD. There might be companies who do business between the U.K and Australia who are trying to reduce their exposure to once currency and buy or sell the pair in order to minimize currency conversion risks.

Then there are a multitude of traders with different strategies. I'm including algorithms within this group as well. Everyone is buying and selling at different time frames with different time horizons and with different intentions. My point in explaining all of this is that there is no central committee of bears or bulls that decides which way the prices ought to go.

It's all organic and it happens in real-time. Everyone, with the exception of those driven by business needs, is busy reading the conditions and how they'll play out. In other words, everyone is placing orders all the time trying to figure out which way the majority of the market is leaning.

Imbalances

Once the signs are evident that the majority of market participants are tilted in one direction, everyone piles in into that direction and this creates an imbalance. The traders who are assuming the other side of the market will test this and if they find that the imbalance is too large, they promptly join the other side of the market.

This is why there is no such thing as a permabull or permabear when it comes to trading. Anyone who calls themselves this is just being ignorant. There is a right side of the market to align yourself with and the wrong side. The trending direction is the right side unless the market happens to be in a large range that signals the formation of a trend in the opposite direction.

Trends are born within these ranges and in fact, their initial portion often form the latter portions of the range. It can be tough to spot the exact candle from where a trend begins but you don't need to do this in order to be successful. Look at Figure 3 from the previous chapter once again.

If price breaks out above that resistance level and if the uptrend continues, it is likely that the strong upward push that occurs from the bottom of figure 3 will be classified as being a part of the new uptrend. However, until that trend begins, we keep it as a part of the large range in box 7.

In fact, we only begin trading long if and when price breaks the resistance level at the top of figure 3. In this large range, the process of accumulation is taking place. Accumulation is when the buyers in the market absorb all the sell orders and begin preparing to push prices higher.

In a range that occurs at the end of a bullish trend, it is the sellers who are absorbing all of the buy orders. This is referred to as distribution. The specifics of either of these methods aren't important as long as you know that this is what is going on. Orders are being redistributed and that 50/50 balance in the market is being tilted towards the side that was the underdog all this while.

Characteristics

So, what are the characteristics of a trending move and how can you spot the strength with which it is moving. In other words, what can you do to build an inner ADX of sorts within your brain by just looking at the price charts? The first quality to look at is the extent of the moves.

How far is price moving in the trending direction and how forcefully is it getting there? Strong trends move far and quickly. This means you'll see a cluster of with trend bars and close to no countertrend bars in the trending move. You will see that the trending bars will be large in size without significant wicks or tails.

All of this conveys strength. Weak trends on the other hand witness a good sprinkling of bars that are both in the trend direction and in the countertrend's direction.

The bars will be small and might have wicks and tails. You've already seen an example of a trend so weak that we ended up classifying it as a range.

Look at box 6 in Figure 1. Here prices are trending on the surface of it but look at how price is moving. Look at the number of bars it takes for prices to cover the same amount of ground as a single bar used to previously cover in the trend. Notice how there is a balance between the bullish and bearish bars in this cluster. None of this points towards bearish strength.

Let's take another look at Figure 1 to see if we can spot examples of a strong trending movement. Figure 1 is replicated below.

Figure 4: Figure 1 Replicated

As you've already learned, Figure 1 shows a trend that is weakening with bullish involvement gradually increasing. You've already seen how the ranges exhibit this fact. How do the trending portions reveal this? I want to clarify at this point: The overall trend is made up of both the ranging portions as well as the trending portions.

There is bound to be some confusion since there is no other word I can use to indicate price movements that move in a given direction. In this section I will be differentiating between these two quite explicitly. However, you should not make the mistake of thinking that an overall trend is limited to just those trending portions. Make sure to differentiate between the two in your mind.

Starting from the left of Figure 1, we see that the bearish bars are quite strong. They increase in size and pretty insignificant tails, which indicates that the bears are overcoming bulls quite easily. Notice the distance that these few bars cover. Contrast that with the number of bars in box 1. Box 1 has a greater number of bars but prices don't go anywhere.

The trending portion between boxes 1 and 2 is interesting to examine. Here we have no strong bullish bars and in fact we see a bullish pin bar form as well. However, notice the distance that price falls. Despite no evidence of huge bearish strength, price still manages to cover a distance that is almost equal to the previous trending portion where the bears looked quite strong.

The other thing to notice is that the bearish candles are far stronger as compared to the bullish ones. The bullish pin bar is met with a bearish pin bar in the very next candle and price declines. When evaluating the strength of trend moves such as these, make sure you pay attention to the extent of the move (is it more or less than the previous trending portion?) as well as the comparative strengths of the bullish and bearish candles.

Between boxes 2 and 3, we have further price drops. Again, the number of candles are less but the bars are quite strong. There isn't any bullish presence here. The initial portion of box 3 includes a further price drop and you might be tempted to include that as a part of the trending portion. This is perfectly fine.

Recall from the previous chapter that you don't have to mark the exact candle from where the range begins or where the trending portion ends. The point is to get a feel for the order flow distribution. If this means you want to shorten the horizontal extent of box 3 then so be it.

Box 3 was a significant one when we last looked at this picture. It had the first evidence of bullish pushback. Despite being rejected quite emphatically, it will be interesting to see how the trending portion is affected by this show of presence by the bulls. The portion between boxes 3 and 4 shows that there is one strong bearish candle which will lead you to think that the bears are quite strong.

However, contrast this portion with the portion between boxes 1 and 2. In the latter case (between 1 and 2), the price bars didn't show much strength but prices dropped quite a lot. Here, we have a strong bearish bar but the price doesn't move much. Look at the swing low that this latest trending portion makes and see how it's pretty close to the bottom of box 3.

Box 4's initial portion also includes a drop with another strong bearish bar. Once again, you could add this as part of the trending portion. If you do this, you'll see that the bears are still strong. However, they make the majority of their moves via two large bars. The rest of the bars in this portion are pretty small.

Either way, the trending portion confirms what box 3 told us. The bulls are increasing in strength. It clearly isn't time to switch our bias in the market but increasing bullish pressure should be expected. Moving forward, we can expect prices to move down with less velocity. We might see smaller bearish bars in the trending portions and a large number of bullish bars that what we've seen thus far in them.

The trending portion after box 4 shows that the bears are pretty strong as of this moment. Funnily enough, none of the things that we expected to happen take place. The bearish bars are long and strong. They cover quite a lot of ground. Don't think that the conclusions we just made are wrong though. It takes more than a single trending portion to disprove what the ranges are telling us.

Box 5 promptly occurs and this is the largest range of them all by some distance. Notice that this range occurs right after the bears put on a show of strength. This shows that the bulls are reacting strongly to the bearish pressure. At this moment, the bears are still very strong, and this is probably what causes the long-range to form. Either way, we notice box 5's size and move onto the trending portion that takes place after it.

Here again, we see strong bearish bars but notice that the low this downward move makes is at the same level as the previous low. In other words, prices have not made any progress to the downside despite the bears showing all this strength. The true progress of a bear trend is determined by the distance between the successive swing lows.

In this case, there is almost no progress. There is a slight decline but really, this isn't much to write home about. Why would this happen? The only explanation is that the bulls managed to push prices back into the trend pretty significantly and the bears had to redo whatever it was they did in the previous push down. Notice that the highest point of box 5 almost erases all of the progress that the downswing prior to box 5 made.

As we reach the right-hand side of the chart, we see that price drops in box 6 but it does so in a pretty lethargic manner. We now know that this drop is really part of a bigger range that is forming but how should you approach this if you saw this happening in real-time?

The fact is that you can treat box 6 as both a trending portion or a ranging portion as well. The exact classification doesn't matter. All that matters is that you look at the distribution of bars and their relative sizes.

Box 6 makes it pretty clear that the bears and bulls are equal in strength. There is an almost equal distribution and the size of both types of bars are small.

When I mention the distribution of bars, don't think you need to count individual bars or some such thing. The objective is to get a feel for how the price is behaving. If you see 50 bearish bars and 49 bearish bars, this doesn't mean the bears are in control or some such thing. The idea is to capture information visually.

Much like how you learned to validate pin bar sizes in the previous book, you need to simply look at the way price bars are printing and draw your conclusions.

We know from the previous chapter that the GBPAUD was poised to eventually break out into a bullish trend once this sequence was finished. Let's take a look at that trend to see if we can understand something more about the way trending portions help us.

Bull Trends

Figure 5: GBPAUD Bull Trend

Figure 5 is the eventual bull trend that develops in the GBPAUD. The resistance zone mentioned in Figure 3 is indicated here by the two horizontal lines. You can clearly see how price forms a tight range just below it before breaking into a strong bull trend.

Notice that a significant portion of this trend happens to fall under the large box 7 we had identified in figure 3. The approach to take is to wait until the strong resistance zone is broken and only then switch to a bullish bias. The reasons for this were explained previously. It seems like the incorrect move in hindsight, but this is because we already know that this is a bull trend.

Imagine a scenario where price turned back down from the resistance level instead of breaking out. In this case, maintaining a neutral to bearish stance would have been correct. Besides, it isn't as if taking shorts from the resistance zone would have lost us money. A limit trade placed at the resistance zone would have made us at least 2R rewards multiple times.

Once price breaks out strongly, you can see that this is a pretty strong breakout given the angle at which it moves. There is a very brief period of sideways movement where it retests the high of the huge spike we had discussed in the previous chapter when speaking of box 7.

The trending portions get stronger despite the bearish reaction in the first box. On the right-hand side of this chart, we see that price has moved into a range and bearish participation is unusually high for a trend that is this new.

In the bearish trend we've been looking at thus far, the bulls made an appearance only at the third sideways move. Here, the bears are making an appearance in the first box itself. This tells us that the trend will see significant headwinds. However, the trending portions of this overall move don't really communicate this.

This is why it's important to look at both trends and ranges in combination. Looking at just the trending portions or just the ranges is likely to leave you with an incomplete picture of things. Different trends last for differing periods of time. With some trends, you might see immediate counter-trend participation (like with this bull trend) and with some, it might be a while before the counter-trend traders show up.

The method of looking at trends and ranges applies to every single time frame you can trade. The only difference is how long you'll spend in your trades and how long you'll have to wait for conditions to reveal themselves. IF you're trading the m5, conditions will reveal themselves pretty quickly.

The flip side is that you will need to make decisions just as quickly to keep up with the changing landscape. Generally speaking, the m30 and H1 offer a decent pace for a lot of traders and these are traded in large numbers. Whatever your time frame of choice, make sure you take the time to dissect charts in this manner.

It isn't easy to trade this way in real-time. It takes practice and a lot of time spent on building your skills. Perhaps the biggest barrier to trading this way is the fact that most traders are not used to placing limit orders at support or resistance zones and entering without any indicator input.

You might argue that waiting for a pin bar or a two-bar reversal might increase your chances of success. In response to this, I request you to take a look at all four charts in this book so far. How many instances of price action patterns can you find at the support and resistance zones? How many trades would you have missed by waiting for some kind of price pattern?

The market doesn't care about neat little price patterns. Traders don't sit around waiting for confirmation in this manner. By traders, I mean those who have the money and courage to move markets in this manner. Your chances of success increase massively when you trade in the direction they're trading in.

I'll address this in more detail in the chapter on mindset. For now, let's take a look at some advanced support and resistance principles.

Chapter 4:

Advanced Support and

Resistance

In the previous book, you learned about the different kinds of support and resistance zones you will find in the markets. I'm going to briefly recap those before moving onto some additional characteristics of these zones. The reason for the recap is that most traders have a distorted view of support and resistance.

They often end up marking pretty much every single zone on the chart and the net result is a series of lines all over the place and tons of confusion. This chapter will help you figure out the levels you need to be paying attention to.

Basics

There are three kinds of support and resistance to pay attention to:

1.   Swing points
2.   Place   where   price
   bounces or reacts from repeatedly
3.   Dynamic levels

Using dynamic levels is pretty straightforward. Now that you understand trends better, it should make sense to you. Use dynamic levels only when you see prices moving in a strong manner and forming small ranges. For example, the initial portions of the bear trend in Figure 1 is prime territory for you to enter on a limit from a dynamic resistance level. More often than not this is the 20 EMA. Figure 6 illustrates this.

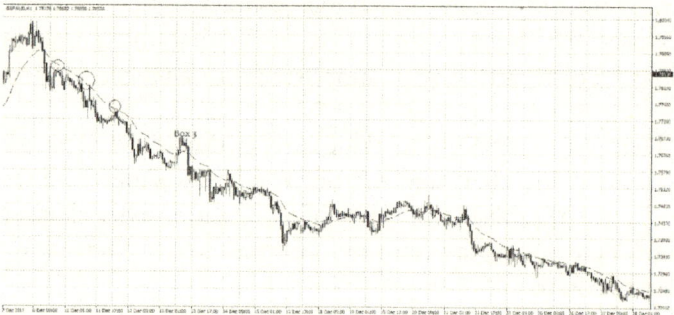

Figure 6: Dynamic Resistance levels at the 20 EMA

The circles indicate areas where you could have entered. Notice that the trending portions are strong in this part of the overall trend and the ranges back this view up as well. Also, notice that the first point where the dynamic resistance level is not respected is at box 3 which is where we first saw bulls make a stand.

Swing points and prior levels that were tested are pretty straightforward to identify. The problem is that there are so many of them. Let's take the same picture as in Figure 6 and look at how the average trader with an imperfect understanding of support and resistance will mark these levels.

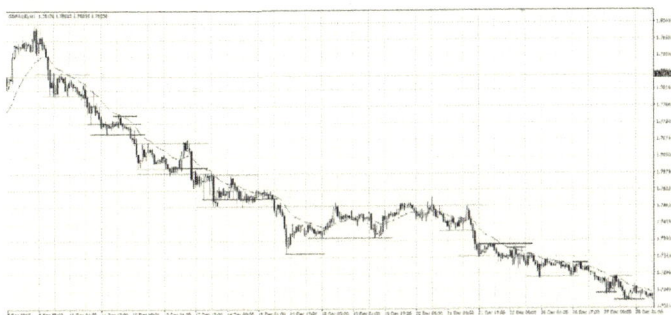

Figure 7: All Support and Resistance Levels Marked

There are a lot of lines marked on the chart in Figure 7. It's pretty hard to say which one is going to be relevant and which one isn't. If price were to make its way back up, a trader who is looking at this sort of a chart would likely have a nightmare trying to figure out which levels they need to pay heed to.

This is a common sticking point for a lot of traders. The fact is that support and resistance levels and the order flow are interrelated. Perhaps the best way to explain this relationship is to use an analogy of a vehicle on a highway.

Force

Let's say you're in a truck that is moving along at 70 MPH on a highway. Now, let's assume that this isn't the real world and that you're in some sort of video game world where random obstacles pop up in front of you. As your truck barrels along, a single column of flimsy-looking bricks appear in front of your truck.

Would this puny excuse for a wall give you much concern? Likely not. You'll probably just power right through it and smash it to pieces instead of trying to avoid it or drive around it. However, what would your reaction be if you were in a tiny bicycle that wasn't moving too fast?

In this case, a column of bricks in your path would give you cause for concern and you would think twice before powering through it. Even if you tried to power through it, it is likely that you won't make it on your first try. The power that the brick wall has to stop you is directly related to your own situation. If you're moving along powerfully, it's not going to register. However, if you're moving slowly, you're going to take notice of it and it will likely halt your progress.

Hopefully, this analogy is making sense to you. The brick wall is the average support and resistance zone that prices encounter on their way in a trend. The truck or bicycle in the analogy is meant to signify the force with which price moves. Large bars and almost no counter-trend presence require a very strong wall to hold price back (Mitchell, 2020). Typically, such levels are present on multiple time frames.

There is another way to look at this. As prices move strongly in a given direction, they're unlikely to need much encouragement to move that way. Think of a vehicle that is held by the tiniest of brakes parked on a downhill slope. A good nudge will likely cause the vehicle to overcome whatever resistance the brakes apply and it will begin rolling downhill.

Prices in trends behave in the same manner. In the early portion of trends where the market is heavily imbalanced in terms of order flow, prices don't need much encouragement to move in their desired direction. They need just a small nudge and this nudge comes from support and resistance levels.

After all, this is where traders lie in wait and it stands to reason that they're the ones who will place orders that will result in the trend continuing or stopping. As the momentum slows down though, prices need even bigger nudges. Bigger in this sense means that a larger number of orders need to be placed and this can happen only if a greater number of traders are present.

Where are the greatest number of traders present? At strong support and resistance levels of course! Thus, the more balanced the order flow is, the more you ought to look at strong support and resistance ones to place your trades. In the earlier portions of trends, you can use weak levels to enter trades. A small swing point or a zone that prie has tested just once or twice in quick succession is more than enough for you to enter.

However, if you see high levels of countertrend participation then you will need to pick stronger levels. If you cannot find strong levels close by, you will need to retreat further back into the price move in order to find relevant zones.

This is an important point to keep in mind. Your objective in trading isn't to just mark the support and resistance zones. It is to determine which is relevant and which one isn't. A seemingly strong zone might be irrelevant thanks to how forcefully price is moving towards it. It will most likely break upon impact.

Conversely, the tiniest of zones might be relevant to enter in the trend's direction since prices are moving with a great deal of force. They don't need much in the way of encouragement or volumes to go in the direction of the trend. Now that we have a better picture of how we need to think about support and resistance, can I clean Figure 7 a bit?

Interpreting Levels

Figure 8: Relevant Levels

The first thing to do is to take stock of how the price is behaving at the moment. Let's assume we're on the right edge of the chart in Figure 8. We've already seen how at this particular moment, we're expecting the bulls to push back strongly against the bears thanks to the order flow balance gradually moving into a state where the distribution is 50/50.

This means that both sides of the market have equal force behind them and as such, we will need to retreat to a strong level to be able to enter a trade with the confidence that prices will likely go our way.

The closest level is the broken support zone at the bottom of the previous range (marked as box 6 earlier). Notice how it was tested from above as well as the bottom. The problem here is that the level hasn't behaved as a great resistance level when it has pushed the price down. The swing downwards is pretty lackluster and if price approaches this level again, we can't be sure as to how the price is going to behave.

Evaluating the strength of this level is pretty straightforward. You simply need to look at the strength of the reactions that have been produced here. Notice the downswing is not very strong. In terms of an upswing as well, while initial bounces were good, the level didn't produce too much in terms of support as price sought to break the level.

All in all, this level is an example of one that is not very strong and is unlikely to hold if tested once again from the bottom. Instead, the thing to do is to retreat to a higher zone. We see such a zone at the top of the range and even this level has behaved as both support and resistance previously.

While its performance as a support level doesn't look very promising, keep in mind that this level existed when the price environment was far more imbalanced. At that point in time, the bears were firmly in control and the bulls had just made their presence known. In such an environment, for a level to hold for as long as it did is commendable.

Notice the number of times it was tested from above. It produced two bounces before the third bounce led to it breaking. Once price retested it from the bottom, it held four times before pushing prices down eventually. All in all, this is a pretty promising level and we would do well to wait here.

Note that despite this level being stronger than the one below it, we don't automatically discard the weaker level. This is because the relevance of the level is a combination of the strength of the level as well as the price environment. If prices behave in a manner that suggests that the bears are still in majority control, the weak level will be relevant.

As such, our analysis suggests that this will not be the case but you never know with the markets. You might end up making a mistake with your order flow analysis. Thus, don't automatically discard weak levels. If prices move to that weak level in an appropriate manner, you could use that level to enter in the direction of the trend.

Another factor to take into consideration is that a level might look weak on your current timeframe but it could be strong when taking multiple timeframes into account. This is best illustrated by looking at what happened with the GBPAUD once it approached these levels from the bottom.

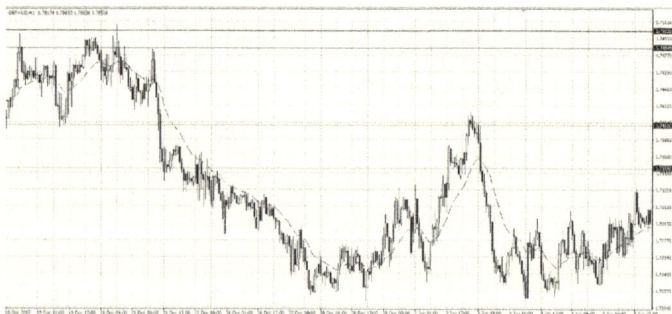

Figure 9: Levels Retested

As you can see from Figure 9, the two resistance zones are marked by the four horizontal lines. We've concluded thus far that the lower zone is weak and the higher zone is strong and that any strong bullish push is likely to be met with resistance by the bears over here

However, Figure 9 tells a different story. The price slams into the lower level as strong as it possibly can and immediately turn downwards. How can such a weak level produce such a strong bearish reaction? Well, the answer is that our original analysis failed to take timeframes into account. Figure 10 tells us the story.

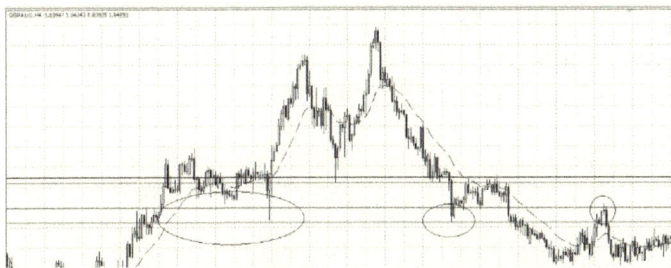

Figure 10: H4 timeframe

Figure 10 is a snapshot of the H4 timeframe which is one level above from the H1. This tells us a very different story from what the H1 told us with regards to the strength of the levels. On the left, you can see the portion indicated by the bigger circle shows a huge upswing right where we've marked our lower level from the H1 time frame.

Looking at this picture, it is evident that the lower zone is the stronger one and that the higher zone, while strong, is weaker than this one. We arrive at this conclusion by solely looking at the extent of the reaction produced and the fact that prices held at this level despite being tested so far apart.

Thus, it makes sense that prices would get held up here when they test this level as a resistance zone. Generally speaking, when you see a V shape formed in prices, it indicates that prices have run into higher-level support or resistance zones. Some traders make the mistake of thinking that these V shapes indicate changes in a trend.

This is untrue. As you've seen, trend changes take place over a long period and occur within a large range.

As you can see, figuring out which support or resistance level is relevant isn't as hard as it seems when you first approach the topic. Take the price environment into account and move forward from there. At this point, you now have three major factors that will help you decipher what's going on with the market.

You've learned how to evaluate ranges. You've learned how to evaluate trends and lastly, you now know about relevant support and resistance levels and how they're determined. It's now time to put all of these together to see how you can trade the markets successfully.

Chapter 5:

Putting it All Together

This chapter is going to walk you through a series of trades in an instrument. I will be using all of the techniques you've learned thus far. As you'll see there is no special or secret sauce that I'm using. It's just plain analysis of the markets in the manner I've shown you thus far.

Also note that other than the 20 EMA, I am not using any other indicator to help me make any decisions. The fact of the matter is that you don't need any such tools to trade. All you need to do is to evaluate the price chart.

USDJPY

The instrument of choice for this chapter is the USDJPY. At the very least it will provide a welcome change from staring at the GBPAUD charts over and over again! Here is the current scenario in this pair. The trading time frame of our choice is the H1. This makes the H4 the higher time frame. We begin by taking stock of things on the H4 and then move onto the H1. Figure 11 is the current H4 scenario.

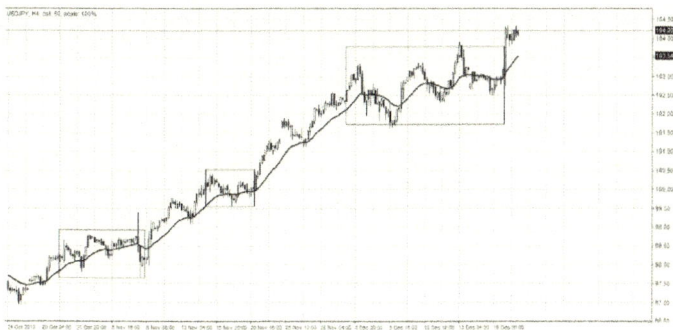

Figure 11; USDJPY H4

We see that there is an uptrend in this instrument and that the ranges are getting bigger. All in all, it looks like the bears are getting back into the market. Again, we don't know when the uptrend will end but it seems unlikely that it is going to last for too long after this point. Let's look at Figure 12 to see what the H1 looks like.

Figure 12: USDJPY H1

The H1 is much more volatile as you can see. Prices have just broken out of a large range where bears made their presence known pretty strongly. As such, we can assume that the bulls and bears are pretty close to parity in terms of order flow distribution. This means that we need to consider strong support levels as being relevant.

There are no resistance levels that present themselves as being relevant at this point in time. The support zone at the bottom of the latest range is the best candidate thus far and we mark that level accordingly. Let's now move forward and see what happens and where we can enter our trades.

Figure 13: USDJPY H1

Moving ahead a little we can see that price is still in a sideways move and is moving towards the bottom. At this point we need to evaluate which level promises the lowest level of risk in terms of trade entry. The swing point marked by the circle seems to be a candidate.

It is a support level at the very least but is it a good one? It does seem to be at the same level as the previous peak that price made but judging by the rather weak reaction price had from this level, it's probably best to stay away from this level. We know that the bears are strong at the moment and need to look at a level that is stronger. As such we maintain our previous view that the lower support zone is the one to park ourselves at.

Figure 14: USDJPY

As we move forward some more, we can see that price did hit the level we decided to ignore and actually gapped upwards. It has since then moved in a sideways manner and is again approaching that same level. Let's take stock of what this means for us. First off, just because price behaved in this manner doesn't mean that our analysis was wrong.

There are a lot of variables that go into determining which way prices move and it is impossible to be 100% correct all the time. Having said that, we should always look for strong evidence of support and resistance levels, no matter what our previous opinion was. As of the present moment, as indicated in this chart, that level is indeed a good one. It has now produced two reactions, with the second one being quite strong.

If the price does reach this level once again, it is a good idea to place a buy limit near the level and aim for a profit. For ease of illustration, I'm going to target a 2X multiple with all of these trades. Figure 15 indicates what happened a few bars later.

Figure 15: Trade in the USDJPY

The highest dotted line indicates the profit target for this trade while the middle line is the entry. The lowest dotted line is the stop loss level for this trade. As you can see, you need to place your limit a few pips above the support zone and stop loss a few pips below it. In this case, I have opted for a wider than normal stop-loss since there is a significant bearish presence in the market. This means that prices are likely to swing to a greater extent. This trade eventually goes for a profit.

Figure 16: H4 in the USDJPY

Figure 16 shows how our trade went for a profit and also shows what happens after that. The H4 chart provides a clearer picture of things which is why I've opted for it in this case. You can see that prices are approaching our previous trade's entry level quite strongly. The question is: Should we enter at this level once again?

Given the force with which prices are moving towards it, it's probably best to wait and watch. The way this chart looks, we're clearly in a range and prices might be shaping up to form a large range that flips the trend in the other direction with the lower support zone being the base of the range.

If it does happen to pass, then the higher level is pretty insignificant since in this time frame it hasn't produced any significant reaction. Also notice how small the bullish bars are compared to the current bearish ones. It seems as if the bears are preparing to push prices down pretty swiftly. It's also worth pointing out that on the H1 time frame, the higher level is the point where we'll flip our bias from bullish to bearish.

The reason for this is that this level is the one that has produced the most significant upswing in recent times. If the price does break past this level, we'll have a situation where we're bearish in the H1 but neutral/sideways in the H4. This is perfectly normal. Timeframe biases clash with one another all the time. You can choose to trade short in the H1 but understand that the H4 is the timeframe that will prevail.

This means that any short on the H1 will eventually meet bullish pushback in an unpredictable manner since the higher time frame is an environment where both sides of the market have equal strength. In this particular scenario, it is best to stay away from placing any bearish or even bullish trades on the H1 since we need a very strong support level to be able to contain these levels of bearish pressure.

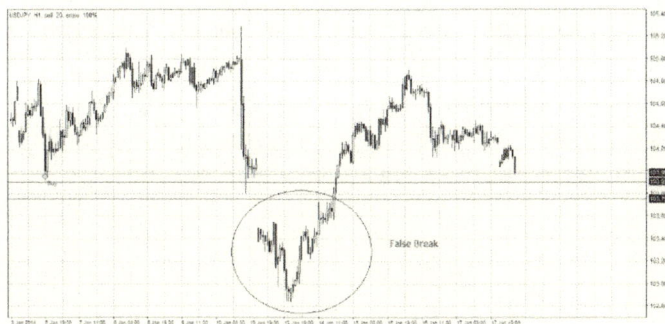

False Break

Figure 17: H1 on the USDJPY

Figure 17 shows what happened as the price approached the higher support zone on the H1. It broke through quite violently and actually resulted in a gap being formed. Our bias would have switched to bearish on this time frame but given that we're staying away from bearish trades thanks to disagreement with the H4, we don't place any short trades.

This is a good decision since the price immediately and strongly moves back up the support zone. This means that the break below the support zone was a false break. A false break or false breakout is when price dives below a support one or moves above a resistance zone and then immediately moves back in the other direction.

These occur primarily because one side of the market, in this case the bulls, could not contain the bears due to excessive bearish pressure. Instead, they had to dig deeper and managed to overcome bearish pressure. As such, given this formation, we place a long trade at this level once again. Since prices are above the support zone, we're once again bullish. Given that the H4 is neutral, it's probably best to place our stop loss a bit closer and reward closer as well since price will likely swing away from our reward level before it hits it.

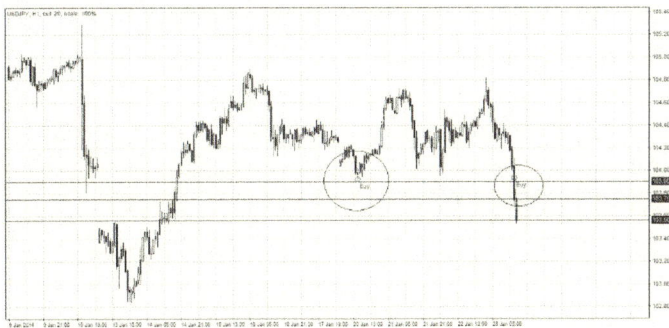

Figure 18: Trades on the H1

The trade that is placed at the level eventually goes for a win. As you can see from Figure 18, prices then moves sideways and then re-approaches the level once again. This level is still an important one in this time frame and given how well it has held up thus far, there is no reason for us to doubt that it won't hold once again. As such we place another long trade here.

This time though, the trade goes for a loss and price accelerates once it breaks past the level. This sort of behavior makes a false break less likely. However, we're still not going to trade the bearish side of the market thanks to the H4 exhibiting a bullish to neutral stance at this point. We're better off waiting for the price to form some sort of bottom or for it to reach the lower support zone we had initially marked.

Price does decline swiftly and it eventually smashes into the bottom support level with huge force. This holds even on the H4. If the H4 has exhibited slower progress towards the support level, we could have entered a limit in the H1 time frame. However, given that there is a high level of bearish pressure all around, it's best to wait and see what happens. If prices bounce from here or consolidate above the level, it would be smarter to enter there instead of placing ourselves in front of a freight train.

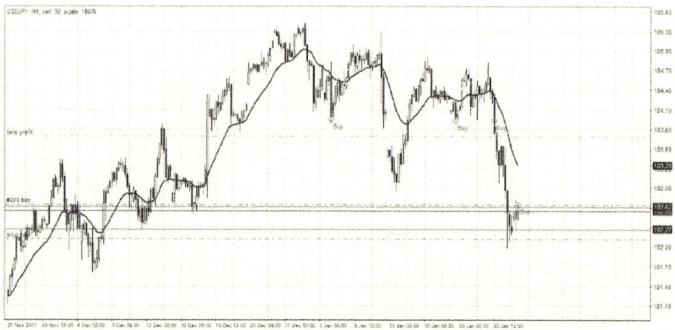

Figure 19: Long Entry H4 USDJPY

Figure 19 is a picture of the H4 situation as price slams into the bottom support zone. As you can see, the bearish bars form tails and price holds at this level to a certain extent. If bearish pressure was strong enough, it would have continued to blow past this level. As such, it seems as if the bulls are holding their own here to a great extent. Given this state of affairs, it's best to enter at this moment. We enter using a market order and place out stop loss below the support level.

The issue here is that the take profit level seems too far away. Prices might turn away from it before they reach there. Either way, we're in a trade now so let's see how it plays out. As it turns out, this is exactly what happens and price does bounce but it falls short of our profit level and hits our stop loss level. Thus far we've placed four trades with two turning out to be losses and two going for wins.

Given that we've been earning at least 2R on our wins and losing R on average, we're still in a decent amount of profit. As price breaks past below this support level, we need to retreat further to find places where it might be challenged. You might be wondering at which point should we flip our bias from bullish to bearish on the H4? In this particular case, it is a bit tricky as Figure 20 illustrates.

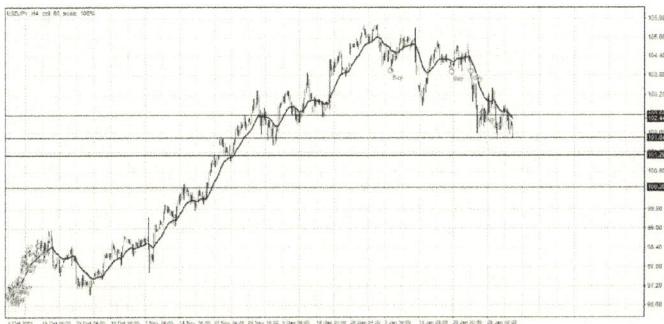

Figure 20: H4 Zoomed Out

Figure 20 is a zoomed out chart of the H4. There are four horizontal lines on this chart. The first two lines from the top represent the old support zone that we had marked as being relevant. The bottom two lines represent a significant level on the daily chart. As such, these two zones are pretty close to one another. If we were to consider the top zone to be the place where we flip our bias, this puts us in conflict with the zone right below it since the D1 traders are likely to push prices back up from there.

Why are we even going all the way up to the D1 in the first place? Aren't we tradin the H1? Well, as it stands right now, we're bearish on the H1 but we're not sure what our bias ought to be on the H4. We were neutral/bullish thanks to the range that was forming. Now that the range seems to have broken, we should be bearish. However, the D1 level poses a problem and might cause the bearish trend in the H4 to flip back upwards.

It might even cause the range to prolong itself further. Thus, our bias if that happened would remain neutral/bullish. All in all, we want to trade the H1 in line with the H4. Given that we're not sure of what the bias on the H4 is, we need the input of the D1 to clarify things.

Since those two levels are close to one another, we would be better off following the cues of the D1 which is the higher level in this case. Since that support zone is so close to the H4 level, we modify our bias only when that D1 zone is broken. Thus, we're still bullish/neutral on the H4 and bearish on the H1. This means we're looking for bullish entries on the H1 as price descends lower towards that strong support zone.

All of this is a lot of information to absorb. It doesn't help that this sort of price action isn't commonly seen in the markets. Usually, the levels where you can flip your bias will line up pretty well with one another across time frames. It just so happens that in this case, everything is a bit tougher.

Moving forward, given the conclusions we've just reached, we remove the lines that mark our old H4 support zone and instead consider the daily level as being more relevant. A point to keep in mind is that the H1 is bearish right now and is headed into a very strong support level. There are two things that can happen here, with a high degree of probability.

The first is that the H1 bearish trend might go into a long range (relatively speaking) at the level and flip back upwards. The other is that it might form a V bottom and flip back upwards. We should be on the lookout for both of these things happening. A V bottom gives us less time to go long and the range gives us more time.

As it happens, price begins to form a range in the support zone. This is good news for us since we can take our time planning our entry. Remember that the H1 trend is most likely to flip at this point since it is at a strong support zone. Therefore, we should expect a range that indicates the end of a trend on H1. The thing to do is to look for a series of higher lows to confirm that a bull trend is about to begin.

Figure 21: Buy Limit on H1

A higher low is precisely what is eventually formed on the H1. Figure 21 shows the new buy limit order we have in place once prices rise. Given the strength with which they're rising, placing them at the closest support or resistance level makes sense. Remember we don't need a strong level to push prices upwards. We have the support of the D1 traders, the H4 traders as well as all the bulls on H1. Towards the left of the picture you can see the result of the previous trade as well that ended in a loss.

As it turns out, we get a little lucky with this trade entry. Prices move away from our desired entry levels but suddenly dip down. They come close to our stop loss level and then rise right back up. They then proceed to hit our profit target on the very next bar.

Figure 22: Entry and Exit

As you can see from Figure 22, this sort of volatility is a stroke of luck. Either way, we bank our profits and move forward with our analysis.

Remember that we're still near the daily support zone and are looking for bullish entries on the H1 so that we're trading in accordance with what the higher time frames tell us. Keep in mind that since the H1 is in a bull trend, you're going to have to read the bearish participation levels as the trend progresses in this time frame.

If price were to make it back to the support level from which we took our last trade, that is near the daily support zone, this would mean that we would have gone through a full bull trend cycle on the H1. We would have seen a trend form (we've already placed and won a trade that took advantage of this), we'll see it weaken and form a range that would give rise to a bear trend.

Prices will then accelerate bearishly before making their way back down to this support zone where they will either form a V bottom or will form an end of trend type range much like the one we just saw. At that point, you should look to enter long once again. Throughout this bullish and bearish cycle, the H4 will be a neutral/bullish environment while the daily will be bullish. Thus, placing any shorts on the H1 is inadvisable.

Let's skip forward and see what happens when prices make it back to the support level. Figure 23 illustrates this.

Figure 23: A V Bottom

Figure 23 makes it pretty obvious that this time around, a V bottom has formed. This means you need to get in on a market order as quickly as possible otherwise, price is likely going to run away from you. This is pretty much what happens as prices rise strongly in a bullish manner.

This is also where I will be stopping this trade walkthrough. As you can see, I've been using the principles we've discussed thus far. It begins with analyzing the higher time frame and then trying to align yourself as much as possible with what is happening in your time frame of choice. If there is a mismatch, stay away from placing any trades.

This chapter will probably be tough for you to follow when you first read through it. I have utilized all of the principles you have learned in this book at various points and to different degrees. In addition to this, I've also prioritized the importance of heeding higher time frame support and resistance levels.

Take your time reading this chapter. You'll find that trading well is not about mechanically applying some formula or indicator. If you still have doubts, go back and look at how many price patterns were produced by price and how much information they could have provided you with regards to the market environment. A single pin bar doesn't tell you much about what has transpired before it does it?

In most cases, there are no price action patterns thrown. Does this mean that the entire order flow of the market is invalid? Clearly, this isn't the case.

Chapter 6:

Other Advanced Strategies

There are many ways to make money in the markets and the global nature of the forex market means that there is no shortage of strategies available for you to implement. In this chapter, I'm going to focus on a few strategies that are not technical in nature but they do work in the markets.

Some of them exist due to a quirk in the way the market is structured and some require advanced technical equipment. I'm not talking about a fancy indicator but am referring to the hardware you use to trade. Let's begin by looking at one of the most famous and popular forex trading strategies.

Positive Carry

When you trade FX, you're buying one instrument and simultaneously selling another. After all, this is what a currency pair is. Your broker handles this as a single instrument trade and passes it onto their liquidity provider who is an interbank dealer (Parker, 2020). This is where things get tricky.

There is no physical instrument called the EURUSD for example. You can't hold it or trade with it physically. The two components of that instrument exist however and in order to facilitate your trade, the LP has to execute your trade accordingly. For example, if you're long the EURUSD, then the LP ultimately buys Euros and sells USD. Your order isn't the only one they're handling and they end up buying and selling millions, sometimes billions, of currencies in a single day.

The thing about buying a currency is that you will be paid interest on it. This is because the central bank that governs the currency fixes certain interest rates that are applicable to that currency. For example, in America, the U.S Federal Reserve Bank or The Fed, governs interest rates. This is the rate at which banks and dealers can borrow U.S Dollars from the American government.

When your LP buys a currency on your behalf, they're simultaneously lending it out to someone else. This act of lending creates the need for an interest payment, due to the owner of the currency (in this case you). The interest rate payable is a few points higher than the central bank rate for that currency.

Thus, in your EURUSD long trade, you will earn interest on one leg of the trade since you're buying the currency and you'll have to pay interest on the USD leg since you're selling it. If you short the EURUSD then you'll pay interest on the Euro and earn interest on the USD.

The interest earned is not fully passed onto you. The LP takes a cut as does your broker. As far as your broker is concerned, this is free money for them and it's unreasonable to expect a broker to pass this up. They'll take a small cut of your interest payment and pass the rest onto you.

Whenever you enter a position, you will have to either pay interest or you will earn interest on a net basis. If the interest earned on the euro is greater than the interest you pay on the dollar, you will make money by simply staying in the trade (Hall, 2020). If the dollar requires a higher payment than the euro provides, you'll pay money to remain in the position.

Your broker will administer this every 24 hours and will accordingly credit or debit your account. Given the way world economies currently are, the differences in interest rates are pretty small. For example, even if you earn money on the trade, you'll gain perhaps a half of a cent on a single lot overnight. This really isn't much of a payment.

However, if the difference between the interest rates governing the two currencies are large enough, you could earn a substantial amount of cash. This is precisely what used to happen in the early portion of the previous decade with the USDJPY. The American economy was booming, following the dotcom crash while the Japanese economy was deflating.

Deflation is when prices of goods in an economy decrease instead of increasing. You might think this is a good thing but it hints at economic malaise. It simply means that the economy is not producing enough goods and the overall level of spending and economic activity is decreasing. A side effect of this is a crash in real estate values as well as the value of the currency.

I'm simplifying a complicated macroeconomic concept here. The relationship between these things is not one to one. As a trader, all you need to know is that deflation is a bad thing while inflation is good. Too much inflation is bad since this means prices will rise way too fast for the economy to be able to keep up with them. For example, the average inflation rate in the U.S has always hovered around 2.5% this decade.

The Japanese central bank had a huge problem on its hands and in an effort to jumpstart the economy, they reduced interest rates constantly until they hit rock bottom by the turn of the millennium. None of this was having an effect so the interest rates stayed right where they were (Hall, 2020).

Meanwhile, the U.S was booming and interest rates kept increasing. This is a natural consequence of a booming economy. Soon the gap between these currencies became large and as a result, a great trading opportunity was born. Investors could buy USD and sell Yen (buy the USDJPY) and earn a huge sum of interest overnight.

The differential was so large that the interest payments would overcome any losses in the trade position. In other words, the trade was being 'carried' by the high-interest payment from the USD leg of the trade.

How to Trade it

Traders back then would hold their shorts indefinitely as long as interest rates prevailed at their existing levels. Other traders would initiate a short position a few hours before their broker processed payments and would then cover the trade once the payment was transferred, thus holding onto the trade for a few hours at the most.

This reduced the risk of carrying a short for a long period of time and limited downside trade risk. These days, the way to implement the carry trade is the same. All you need to do is find a currency pair that has a high-interest differential and go long on the currency that pays the higher rate.

There are a few obvious risks to this strategy. The first risk is that it is extremely dependent on what fiscal policy is deemed appropriate by the central banks of the countries involved. If interest rates change this will directly impact your trade. The other risk has to do with the general climate of the world these days.

Historically central banks didn't mind fixing high-interest rates. Since the credit crisis of the previous decade though, interest rates all around the world have been at historically low levels, with some economies shifting to negative interest rates (the government pays you to draw a loan, as twisted as it sounds).

Japan has been maintaining a low-interest rate for decades now, but the picture has dramatically changed with other economies. The differentials aren't as great as they used to be and you will need to take into account the gain or loss on the actual trade since the interest payment cannot cover losses anymore (Chen, 2020).

The quest to find high differentials has pushed traders into the area of the exotics and these are fraught with risk. For one thing, you're exposing yourself to extremely volatile spreads. For example, the USDZAR (South African Rand) has a high differential. However, the spread is so large that you'll end up with a guaranteed loss on the trade if you're looking to simply enter and exit to capture the payment.

Holding onto this for the long term is even riskier since liquidity could always disappear overnight. This usually brings traders right back to the JPY pairs. Currently, the AUDJPY is the one in favor but again, the position's profit and loss need to be taken into account.

Earning a carry isn't as simple as it used to be, but it is possible. If you find the right conditions, you can go long on the AUDJPY and earn a decent interest rate to augment your trade profits. There are many who will tout the carry trade as being a risk-free option but this is not the case at all.

It used to be the case, but it doesn't apply any more thanks to the fiscal environment the world finds itself in. With smart trade management though it is possible to earn a carry. Lastly, you'll find a lot of so-called traders automatically refer to the long USDJPY as being the 'carry' trade. Hopefully, you can understand now why this is a wrong label to apply.

Announcements and Fundamentals

Currencies are greatly affected by the fundamental factors that influence the economies they're tied to. In the case of the U.S dollar, the most important factors affecting the currency are interest rate announcements, general election results, and the Non-Farm Payrolls report (NFP). Of these, the NFP is the best way to earn a great return.

The reason for this is that interest rate announcements don't often tend to produce huge surprises. Responsible central bank governors prepare markets in advance of their announcements and the release of the interest rate doesn't come as a surprise. Thus, while volatility might increase, it doesn't do so greatly. The general election comes by once every four years and this is a long time for you to wait to place a trade.

The NFP, on the other hand, is released on the first Friday of every month at 8:30 A.M EST. As far as forex releases go, it is a big event. Markets experience huge swings in volatility and the prospect of making a huge profit in the matter of a few minutes isn't unrealistic (Chen, 2020).

The report itself is a snapshot of the current state of employment in the United States. A high unemployment rate is a cause for concern for the Fed and this often results in them easing monetary policy. In other words, they lower interest rates. The idea is that with money becoming cheaper to borrow, this will inject more cash into the economy and as a result, more jobs will become available thanks to greater economic activity.

One of the results of this is that the value of the U.S Dollar as compared to other currencies reduces. This is because lower interest rates mean lower yields of investors. After all, owning the U.S Dollar now results in a lower interest payment. This means there are better investment options out there and a flood of selling ensues.

As a result, supply increases and the dollar drops in value. Thus, a better than expected NFP number is considered bullish and a worse than expected NFP number is bearish. This means you would buy the dollar in every pair you choose to trade. Thus, you would short the EUR USD and buy the USDJPY and so on.

Following the NFP is a tough task. This is because it is close to impossible to generate the number that is most expected from a retail trader's standpoint. Thus, the best thing to do is to simply get a feel for what the expected number is and align yourself accordingly once the number is released.

Even this isn't a perfect strategy since the market will become extremely volatile and spreads will widen. Thus, you're going to find that your orders might not be filled or you might not be able to get in at attractive prices. Despite this, some traders do very well by adopting positions in pairs ahead of time and betting in one direction.

Trading the NFP well is all about managing your downside risk. A regular stop loss will not work in such instances since the market is volatile and your stop levels could be jumped. Instead, the best way to implement your strategy is to use options.

How to Use Options

Typically, FX traders don't dabble in options since the world of options trading is a completely different one. There, volatility is what counts and price moves are beside the point. However, there are many benefits to trading options when it comes to implementing a strategy that takes advantage of a move in the markets post NFP announcements.

The first strategy is to bet directionally using puts or calls. This way, you eliminate the risk of the market jumping your stop because your risk is limited to the premium you pay for your option. You can always let it expire worthless. Whatever you do, do not write an option to trade the NFP release since volatility jumps off the charts in such scenarios.

Betting directionally can make you money but it isn't the smartest play here. What you really want to be trading is the expansion in volatility and the best options strategy to implement is either a straddle or a strangle. This is when you will buy an out of the money (OTM) call and an OTM put. In the case of a straddle, your strike prices will be close to the market price while in the case of a strangle, they will be further away.

Keep in mind that option premiums will take the additional NFP volatility into account so you will need to enter your position a few weeks prior to the NFP announcement. Keep in mind that the premium prices you pay for your options will increase the amount by which the pair has to move in order for you to break even.

Straddles and strangles don't require any prior knowledge of the Greeks or any other advanced options terminology. You know well in advance that volatility is going to be introduced so you simply go long volatility. Whichever direction the market moves in, you will make money.

Macroeconomic Factors

Using macroeconomic factors isn't a strategy as much as it is a philosophy unto itself. This is how a lot of hedge funds trade and there is no set formula you can apply. For example, you could analyze the interest rate scenario in Europe and determine that the current levels of debt make certain exchange rates untenable.

This could lead you to go long or short certain currencies. Perhaps the most famous bet of this kind was the one George Soros placed when he shorted the Pound (Hall, 2020). Another great example of this was when the financial journalist Jim Grant reasoned that negative interest rates plus the rising debt situation in Switzerland make the fixed exchange rate of 1.3 Euros for 1 CHF unrealistic. The only way forward was to remove this floor and to let the Euro fluctuate freely against the CHF.

The Swiss National Bank removed the floor a few months later and the price of the EURCHF pair promptly crashed making traders millions in a few seconds (and also losing those amounts in the same amount of time). The point here is that there are many complex macroeconomic factors at play. If you feel you have an edge here instead of within technical factors, then by all means go ahead and trade these.

Some instruments have peculiar behavior thanks to the presence of floors or minimum exchange rates along with maximum exchange rates. A good example of this is the Hong Kong Dollar to USD. The HKD is governed by the Hong Kong Monetary Authority or HKMA. HKMA has prescribed a band within which the HKD will exist. This creates a floor and a ceiling for the currency. In other words, it moves in a predictable range (Hall, 2020).

You might think that buying the low and selling the high is the thing to do here. The problem with thi strategy is that brokers are wise to it as is every trader in the market. Therefore, spreads are high and unless you get lucky, you're not going to get a good price. Then there's the pair itself. No one trades it since everyone knows where it ought to go.

Therefore, the pair barely moves and takes months to float from one end of the range to the other. The smarter thing to do is to instead trade the CFD associated with the Hang Seng Index (HSI) which is the stock market index of Hong Kong. Greater cash inflows into the HKD means bullishness in the HSI. This means when you see the USDHKD pair declining, the HSI is probably increasing in value.

There is a very strong correlation between these two instruments and you can use the currency pair's movements to time your entries into the HSI. Another option (literally) would be to buy options on the HSI and trade those to limit your downside CFD risk. These kinds of situations exist around the world and getting to know them by examining the macroeconomic factors surrounding them is the best way forward.

There is no fixed strategy I can provide you with unfortunately. However, great opportunities do exist.

Chapter 7:

Advanced Risk

Management

In the previous book you learned all about why risk management is so important. More importantly, you learned why it is so difficult for us to understand trading properly because of how we think about success in trading. We equate being right with success, thanks to the way we've been conditioned from school onwards.

However, success in trading is a combination of being right as well as making sure you really cash in when you're right and limit your losses when you aren't. This creates a profitability combination that involves your win rate as well as your average win and loss sizes.

True risk management goes a bit beyond that. While those basic metrics will keep you on the right side of profitability, in order to start making more money you will need to monitor a few more metrics. More importantly, if your aim is to trade professionally, monitoring these metrics are a matter of course for you since every prospective investor will ask you about these.

Let's begin by taking a look at how your trading journal is set up.

Journal

Most traders' trading journal contains a list of the trades they placed and that's it. There's no information about what they saw or the rationale behind the trade's placement. The profit and loss are recorded but this hardly reflects what went right with the trade. After all, you can do everything wrong in trading and still make money.

The following sections will help you figure out what parts of your trades you need to be recording at the very minimum.

Entry Information

You need to be recording the entry date and the entry prices at the very least. In addition to this, you should also be saving a screenshot of the market as you enter your trade. Some traders go so far as to record their entire trading session and then review it later. A video recording is extremely helpful since it will illuminate any behavior you might not notice within yourself.

Reasons for Entry

What was it that you saw in the market that prompted an entry? There are two approaches to recording this. The first is to use a structured format of bullet points or a list of some sort that you fill out every time you enter a trade. This is pretty helpful during your review time when you'll be able to easily see all the necessary information that led you to make your decision.

The downside is that it does limit your ability to express discretionary reasons for entry. You'll find that the list or framework binds you and you'll end up recording less information. This is where the second method of entry comes into play. This is to record a free form statement of what you saw. The downside of this method is that you're likely to vomit stuff out that you might not be able to figure out later.

Finding a balance between the two approaches is what works best. Remember to include all appropriate information and at the end of your trading session, make annotations on your chart that accurately reflect what you saw. If you felt that a particular level was strong on the higher time frame, include a snapshot of the higher time frame as well.

Mental State on Entry

This is something a lot of traders ignore. You need to turn your trading journal into a mental state journal as well. Record your thoughts upon trade entry. I'm not talking about the rational but what your emotions are in that moment. If you think the setup isn't that great, record it. If you think this one is an absolute home run, then record that as well.

This is especially important for you to review since you'll likely find that you will make a lot of judgments on how your trade ought to be before you place it. Upon review you'll likely find that the most terrible looking setup went for a win and the great-looking one went for a loss.

These emotions tend to wreak havoc on your mental state. You might find that you're needlessly beating yourself up before a trade thanks to them and none of your beliefs have any grounding in reality. In addition to this pay attention to your general mental state prior to beginning your trading session.

This ties in with your preparation routine and I'll address this in detail in the next chapter. Trading when you're feeling anxious about other events in your life or when you're going through a difficult time is counterproductive. You'll only end up making things worse and you will increase the odds of losing money.

Exit Information

You need to record the date and time of your exit as well as the price at which you exited. Some traders ignore the time aspect of the exit but you want to record this in order to calculate certain metrics that you'll learn about shortly. In addition to the exit date and price, you need to capture a screenshot of your exit.

Again, if you have a video recording of both yourself and your screen upon exit or the moments prior to it, this will be extremely helpful. This is particularly relevant if you decide to day trade. This is a fast-moving environment and your mind will be under stress. Traders tend to make poor decisions towards the end of their trading sessions thanks to fatigue and the timestamp will help you figure out if there's any pattern here.

Reasons for Exit

For most traders the reasons for exit are straightforward. Many traders practice the set and forget the methodology of trade management. In this system, a trader simply sets a profit target and a stop loss and lets the market take them out of the trade. Throughout the process, the trader does not tinker with either the stop loss price or take profit levels.

In case you happen to practice active trade management, then you will need to describe what you saw and why you exited your trade in detail. Annotate the exit screenshot so that there are no doubts as to what you saw and what you were interpreting in real-time.

Mental State on Exit

Just like with the entry you want to record your thoughts down in your journal once you exit your trade. Don't place any filters on what you're feeling in that moment and record it all down. If you're recording your trade sessions, then a video journal of it will be extremely helpful.

The exit tends to bring out a lot of emotion in traders since this is where you will get to know whether you've made a profit or a loss. If you're on a losing streak you will likely find that your mind begins to expect a loss on the next trade thanks to recency bias. Monitoring your mental state for these sorts of clues is extremely helpful.

Profit and Loss

This is quite an obvious thing to record. Note down the amount of money you made or lost in the trade. Even better, record the profit and loss as a percentage of your account. This will help you quickly determine where you're following your reward to risk ratio properly or not.

For example, if you've decided to risk 0.5% per trade and are targeting a 3R reward at the very least, your losses should be around or less than 0.5% and your rewards should be at 1.5% of your account balance. Any major deviations from this is a red flag and you can instantly spot what you need to work on.

Trade Review

A lot of traders take the trade review process for granted. What I mean is that they think that reviewing their prior week's trades at the end of the week is enough and some even treat it as a chore. The thing with the trade review is that you need to structure it with as much care as you would your trading session.

Most traders simply take a look at their trading journals, look at their screenshot, write down some stuff about what they could do better and leave it at that. This is better than nothing I suppose but it doesn't take into account the various factors you need to watch out for during review.

The most important factor that traders ignore is the amount of time that passes between the exit and the review. If you exited a trade late on Friday and review it on Saturday, this is unlikely to give you any sort of feedback. Furthermore, the time frame you trade in also determines how much of a gap there needs to be between your exit and review session.

Let's look at the things you need to do and incorporate it as a part of your review process.

Timing

This is perhaps the most important one. You need to leave enough of a gap between your exit and the review session for your trades. The reason for this is very simple. If there isn't enough of a gap, you're going to view pretty much the same set of bars as you did when you entered the trade.

Real feedback is gained once the market has moved forward by a suitable number of bars and until this happens there is no point in reviewing the technical aspects of your trade. For example, you might have placed a trade thinking you're in a trend but are actually in the beginning of a range.

If you were to review this trade, from a technical aspect, a few bars later the range is unlikely to have made itself evident. The point here is that you need to give the market enough time to progress so that you can gain adequate feedback. Keep in mind that this applies to both wins and losses.

You can get lucky in trading and do all the wrong things and still end up with a win. This is why it is important to allow the market to move forward by a decent amount before reviewing your trade. With all of this in mind, when should you review your trades? The best way to handle the review process is to do it on a rolling basis.

This means you will need to review some of your trades every day once your trading session is complete. The higher the timeframe you trade, the longer the gap ought to be between your exit and review. If you're day trading or trading any time frame up to the M30 (not including it), you need to be reviewing your trades daily.

A daily review of trades on the m1, m5, and m15 makes sense due to the large number of bars that will be printed every day. You don't want to delay the review by leaving it for the end of the week because you're likely to forget the exact conditions and reasoning for entry, even if you noted in your journal precisely. Review the previous day's trades once your current session is done.

When it comes to the m30 and H1 time frames, a weekly review is acceptable. Keep in mind that the review needs to be a rolling one so it's not as if you'll be setting aside a single day to review your trades. Depending on the number of instruments you choose to trade, the number of trades to review could be small or large. Either way, the volume of trades you'll take on these time frames will be far less than what you'll take on the lower ones.

When trading the H4 and above, deciding a review period is tricky. First off, it is unlikely that you will be trading the D1 too often. Most traders tend to stop at the H4 time frame due to the ample swing trading opportunities it provides. Either way, take into account that the H4 will print just 20 bars over the course of a week. That isn't enough market action for you to review.

Therefore, a period of at least two weeks has to be in place for you to review your trades. The downside of such a long wait between trade placement and review is that you might forget the precise rationale behind the trade entry. This makes journaling even more important. My suggestion is to record your trade entries and maintain a spoken journal on video as well as a written one. The video will provide the exact thought process and will fill any gaps that your words create.

Again, this is a rolling review period. However, given the relatively small addition of bars that will take place over the course of a week, you can allocate a day on the weekend to review. See what works best for you.

Process

There are two steps to your review. The first is to review your mental execution and the next is to look at your trade execution. Given the delayed nature of reviews on the higher time frames, the question arises: Should you separate them or conduct them together? For example, on an H4 trade, should you conduct a thorough mental execution review at the end of the week or should you wait for the two week period before reviewing this along with the technical execution?

There's no straightforward answer to this question unfortunately. The simplest method is to do what feels right for you. When reviewing your mental execution here are the things you need to be paying attention to:

1. How well did you prepare for the session?
2. What was your state of mind prior to beginning?
3. Did you execute all the things you needed to do prior to the session?
4. What was your mental state in session outside of your trades?
5. What was your mental state like on trade entries?
6. What was it like on exits?
7. Did you execute everything you needed to do post-trade exit?
8. Did you do everything you needed to do after the session was finished?

You can give yourself a score on a scale of one to 10 in each of these categories. This will bring some objectivity into the whole process. Remember the mental review is not about how well you read your entry cues and analyzed the markets. It's all about the quality of your preparation and how well you handled the movements in the market as your trades went towards a profit or a loss.

You might be wondering what point number seven above is all about. What do you need to do after you've exited the trade? I'll cover this shortly when discussing the metrics you need to be keeping a track of.

When it comes to the technical review the things to watch out for will depend on the strategy you implement. With regards to the strategy I have shown you in this book here are the things you need to review:

1. Did you begin with the higher time frames?
2. Did you mark the important ranges?
3. Did you evaluate the ranges to get a feel for the order flow distribution?
4. Did you look at the trending portions to see if this distribution was being backed by trend behavior?
5. Did you identify the key S/R level?
6. Did you take note of any higher time frame levels present?
7. Did you map out your possible entry points ahead of time?
8. Did you plan your stop loss level placement?
9. Were your take profit orders placed at the right levels or were they too far away?
10. Did you risk the correct percentage of your account on entry?
11. Did you manage the trade well as per your plan? If set and forget, did you tinker with your trade before the exit?

12. Did the exit go according to what you planned? Why or why not? I'm talking about the exit levels here and not about situations like planning for a profit and taking a loss instead.

13. If your trade went for a profit, did you earn the correct multiple of your risk?

You can combine some of these points with one another if that makes it easier for you. The objective here is to fully review each and every portion of your technical strategy.

Conclusion

Combining the two portions of your review process will give you insights into what you need to do better. It is best to jot these down as reminders prior to your next trading session. If there are some technical adjustments you need to make begin practicing these before your next session. If the adjustments are big, see if there's any way you can suspend trading for a few days until you manage to install this through the scaling plan I outlined in the previous book.

In case you haven't read the previous book, here's how it works. You implement any changes in a simulation first. You then practice it on demo and only then do you move to live trading. Needless to say, you won't progress in this plan until you've ascertained that you're able to make money with these changes. There wouldn't be any point to implementing them otherwise.

Given that you will be conducting these every day (in most cases), you'll have a steady stream of feedback for you to implement. If you feel as if the changes you need to make are too many or that your brain is unable to process all of them at once, suspend trading live and take some time off to digest all of them.

Trade Processes

When we talk about trading, we rarely talk about the processes we need to execute in order to carry it out successfully. We think of our technical strategies and stop there. However, the degree to which you can successfully execute your mental processes before, during and after the trade will boost your confidence and results dramatically.

Remember that trading a chaotic system. I outlined this in detail in the previous book in this series when talking about how you need to think about your results. The individual results don't matter and neither should you care about them. Instead, your focus should be on the process and how well you execute it.

What is the trading process exactly? Your entry signal is just a part of it. In fact, it is the smaller part of it. Your trade process for the next day begins when you go to sleep the previous day. Your lifestyle affects the way you trade and you should monitor the various factors that affect your mental wellbeing.

Before Trading

I've already covered the aspects of your lifestyle that you need to keep your eye on in my previous book. Things such as your quality of sleep, diet and exercise are good practices not just for trading but for life in general. There are a variety of resources out there that will help you align your lifestyle in a healthy manner and you should do your best to follow those practices.

There is an important aspect of trading that often gets overlooked and this is practice. Traders often spend so much time live in the markets that they forget to take time off to hone their skills and expose themselves to even more varied conditions. The fact is that you need to master quite a few skills as a trader to be successful.

You're not going to be great at all of them the moment you begin trading. This would be unrealistic to expect. In case you're wondering which skills you need to master to trade successfully, you can take a look at the review checklists in the previous section. All of those points represent everything you need to have in order to make large amounts of money over the long term.

As you can see it's a pretty long list! This is why practice is important. Unlike other endeavors, traders don't need to spend too much time practicing. This is because trading live money tends to provide a lot of lessons of its own. However, this doesn't mean you should ignore it.

Practicing well is an art by itself. Don't make the mistake of thinking that your weaknesses should be the only one you should target while practicing. Practice the skills you're good at as well. Spend at least 15 to 30 minutes each day practicing your skills on a simulator. This way you'll move through a ton of market data quickly and will get instant feedback.

The idea behind practice is to slowly develop your skills to the point where you feel comfortable executing every aspect of them without a second thought. To do this well, it helps to develop a practice plan. You can map out which skills you will practice on which day of the week and focus on that during the practice session.

Another great way to practice and gain feedback is to replay the market session in your simulator once you're done trading. This is especially easy for those trading the lower time frames. Once you're done with your session and necessary reviews, step away from the screen for a while to refresh yourself. Then, take around 30 minutes to run through the bars you saw in that session on your simulator to see what you could have done better and how you could have approached things.

Some of your mistakes will be obvious but don't turn this into a review session or into a session of 'what-ifs'.

Focus on practicing your skills and just executing well. This can be tough to do if you've had a tough session. Generally speaking, if you find that you're not on a mental equilibrium after finishing your session, step away from the trading screen and take a break.

Your practice session should be a part of your pre-trade routine, even if you're practicing the day before by replaying the market's bars. As long as you're rehearsing your skills and are fortifying them, how you choose to do this immaterial. Another way of structuring your practice sessions is to practice different skills in a single session.

You could begin by practicing the skills you're good at, then move onto the things you're not so good at and then end with something you're good at once again. For example, if you're not good at pulling the trigger on your trades but can practice excellent risk management on the ones you do pull the trigger on, place a trade on simulation and risk the right amount. Watch it move towards its end and take the right levels of profit or loss.

Next, play the simulator until you spot a particular setup you think is a good one and practice pulling the trigger. Keep replaying the market until you feel confident enough to simply place the trade without hesitation. It takes time but you'll overcome this fear eventually. End your session by practicing something else you're good at.

Another aspect of pre-trade preparation is visualization. By pre-trade, I'm talking about the moments before you place your order or the ones right after you've placed it and have just entered. These moments are anxiety-filled ones because you'll be hoping for gains and will want to avoid losses.

Overcome this yo-yo of emotions by visualizing a perfect trade. A perfect trade doesn't depend on its outcome. It could be a loss as well. Instead, visualize yourself doing everything correctly and doing everything you can control, perfectly. Over time, your brain will associate the placement of a trade with a calm and serene environment where you're in control and are doing everything perfectly.

After Trading

I've already mentioned one task you need to carry out after you're done trading which is the review. However, right after you exit a trade for a profit or a loss you need to make sure you're entering the relevant information in your journal. This is a very important thing for traders to do and the ones who trade lower time frames are often guilty of neglecting this.

This is because of the fast-paced nature of those time frames. This is why a better idea for these traders is to record their screens and then perhaps jot down the timestamps of their trade entries and exits. Once the session is complete you can then fill in your trading journal with the relevant information by viewing the video at the timestamps.

Initially you're not going to have too many statistics to track since you just won't have enough trades to generate data with. However, once you have at least 100 trades placed live you need to begin to keep track of your trading stats on a weekly basis. You can choose to do this manually or you can use free software like Myfxbook.com to do this for you.

Keep in mind that Myfxbook doesn't connect with every broker out there. If your broker happens to not be on the list, you will need to manually calculate this. If you've signed up for an external platform such as Psyquation or Fundseeder that have their own analytics, it's a good idea to track your own stats.

Reviewing your trading metrics is important since it helps you assess how your progress is moving forward. Let's take a look now at some of the most important stats you need to record with regards to your trading and how you need to interpret them.

1. Max drawdown - Your max drawdown is the maximum amount of money you have lost from a peak to a trough in your account's equity curve. If you wish to trade professionally you need to keep this below 5%.

2. Monthly drawdown - This is the highest drawdown you faced over the course of a month. Aim to keep this below 5%.

3. Recovery time - This is how long it took you to overcome the max drawdown to create a new equity peak. Generally speaking, you want this to be twice as fast as the drawdown time. If it took you three weeks to go from peak to trough, you want to see a recovery curve go from trough to a new peak in at least two weeks or less. Either way, as long as it doesn't take you more than the drawdown time, you're doing great.

4. Sharpe Ratio - This is the ultimate metric in terms of risk-adjusted returns. Too many traders worry about this. Instead just follow good risk management as recommended in this and the previous book and this will take care of itself.

5. Trade times - How long are you spending in winning trades and how long do your losers last? If your average losing time is less than a minute while your winners last for two hours on average, there is information there that you can dig into. Are you stepping in front of too many freight trains and getting run over? Are you not being patient enough with your losers?

6. Stops and Take profit levels - Record the distances of these levels and see if extending them can turn losers into winners. The best

place to do this is right after your trading
session when you replay it.

7. Average risk per trade and reward - As
mentioned in my previous book, these need to
be as consistent as possible. Do not fluctuate
when it comes to this since they'll affect
everything that makes your system successful.

There is no defined way to analyze these metrics. You
will have to look at them and figure out what it is you're
doing wrong. If you find yourself on the wrong side of
drawdown curves for instance, with recovery curves
that are a lot longer than drawdowns, then you'll
perhaps need to take a look at your time spent in
winners and losers. Perhaps you're just taking too many
low probability trades.

Having said that, the most important thing you can do
in terms of ensuring your risk is managed is to just
conduct a good review of your trades. Ensure you're
getting good feedback and practice your skills. Most
importantly, scale into live trading correctly. That act by
itself solves almost every problem a struggling trader
has.

If you're currently trading live and aren't making
money, then scaling back to the simulation level is the
best thing you can do for your trading account. Follow
the steps outlined in the previous book and you'll be
just fine.

Remember that discipline is at the heart of good risk management. Commit to the processes you've outlined, and the money will follow.

Chapter 8:

Mindset

A lot of risk management really comes down to how well you manage your mindset. There are many things you can do to create a bulletproof mindset in trading. Before practicing any of those techniques though you need to understand how your mind works.

This chapter is going to spend some time dissecting your brain. You might wonder why this information belongs in a book on trading, but I assure you, once you learn this stuff, you'll see how you've been sabotaging yourself.

The Two Minds

Here's a fact you might not be aware of: Your brain is actually composed of two smaller brains or minds (Hanson & Mendius, 2009). On a physical level, there is the reptilian brain that is responsible for the most basic parts of our survival. This part of our brain is automatic and doesn't have the ability to think in a reasoned manner.

It simply reacts to whatever is present in front of it and does what it has been programmed to do. Think of a situation when you've been in danger or in potential danger. If you accidentally touched something hot, you didn't let your fingers linger on the hot surface. You immediately pulled them back.

This is a very good thing. If you had to stop and think about what to do in that instant, you would likely have damaged your fingers pretty badly. In contrast to the reptilian brain is the prefrontal cortex of PFC. This is the more evolved portion of our brain and is responsible for all of our reasoning abilities.

When in control, it is able to put a stop to our automatic responses and think about them. For example, if you detect heat in your fingers and if your PFC was somehow in charge, it has the ability to question at that moment: Is the heat real or is it imagined? This is not a real-life situation of course but you get the idea.

The PFC can stop and think and this makes it incredibly powerful. The downside is that it is pretty terrible in survival situations. It tends to get overwhelmed by the reptilian brain and switches off when stress is encountered in the short term.

In the long term, under states of stress, something even worse happens. The PFC begins to normalize stress and starts storing information that sabotages us. Since it reasons that stress is normal, it begins to build habits and dictates your actions in a manner such that more stress is created and you end up making yourself miserable.

Let's consider an example: A trader has had a series of bad beats in the market and this person has not decided to take time away from the screen. She feels that by trading more, she's going to make back all of her losses. As such, she is under stress at the moment and her PFC is learning to associate trading with stress.

It is building habits or modifying them in a way so as to agree with this interpretation. The market meanwhile is random and the trader nets a few wins. This brings her into a state of slightly less stress but the PFC steps in. After all, less stress and trading do not equate to one another. Therefore, it sends out signals that associate worry with the loss of this money.

The trader begins to think that she cannot afford to lose this newly made money because she cannot go back to that old state of stress. The irony is that she is already in it. Thus, the fear of missing out is born, which leads to revenge trading, which leads to losses. All the time the PFC is under the belief that it is doing the right thing. Stress is present and trading is stressful. Everything is perfect!

The PFC stores all of these behaviors and habits deep within itself and soon they become part of the subconscious mind. The mind and the brain can be thought of as being two different things. The brain is the physical structure while the mind is the energy your thoughts carry.

Your mind has two portions to it: Conscious and subconscious. When our trader is learning to associate stress with trading at first, this learning is taking place in her conscious mind. She is aware of the stress and can feel her mood swing. Why doesn't she do anything to stop it? Perhaps her beliefs about trading are incorrect or perhaps her expectations have led her to indirectly believe that stress in trading is good.

Either way, once the conscious mind has learned it well enough, it passes into the subconscious and this is when the habit becomes automatic. Our trader now experiences stress on demand when she sits down in front of her trading screen and it's as easy as tying her shoelaces. She doesn't even need to think about it.

As you can imagine, this is a huge problem. The issue here isn't that the mind has been sabotaging her all this while. It's that she's been teaching her mind all the wrong things about trading habits, unconsciously. Perhaps now you can appreciate why I spent so much time in the previous chapter discussing routines and the process.

By carrying things out in an orderly fashion you're teaching your PFC and subconscious mind eventually that trading is all about order and calm. It's about reasoned execution. This is why you scale into trading live money gradually instead of jumping in before you can swim. The scaling process lets you define the best system for yourself before taking it live.

You have the experience of making money (even if it is on paper) before trading live and your mind already has habits built-in that contradict any stress or fear that might crop up. It's pretty logical when you view it in this manner. Unfortunately, many traders let greed take over and begin with the wrong steps.

What if you feel you are like the trader we just highlighted, who has learned the wrong habits by mistake? How can you unlearn them? Well, the trader learned her bad habits by practicing certain actions. Therefore, it stands to reason that you can learn good habits, and beneficial ones, by practicing actions in line with them.

A lot of these actions were discussed in the previous chapter. Over time, these will have an impact and practicing them right from the simulation stage will build a great base for you. If you recall the scaling plan, you will be placing 1,000 trades in simulation and then trading on demo until you earn a profit at the end of a rolling six month period.

That's a whole lot of habits for you to fall back on! In addition to these, you can also practice the following habits to change your beliefs. The first step in changing a belief is to become aware of it.

Meditation

Mindfulness meditation is a great way to enhance your awareness of your thoughts and surroundings. A great number of hedge fund managers are avid practitioners of meditation. The CEO of Bridgewater Associates, Ray Dalio, has mentioned that he practices mediation for 15 minutes every day. This doesn't sound like a lot. Then again, Dalio manages $100 billion in assets so he probably doesn't have much time to begin with.

If Dalio can find time to meditate for 15 minutes while running $100 billion, you can safely find time as well. Studies have shown that meditation literally changes our brain and the way it is wired (Hanson & Mendius, 2009). In other words, meditation is a great way to enforce calm and stillness on the mind and it helps break hardwired nervous habits.

When you feel overly stressed or as if your mind is running away from you when trading, take a few deep breaths and close your eyes. A better option is to use a meditation app such as Headspace which will help you align your mind once again. Take as long as you need and don't feel as if you need to trade immediately.

Meditation is perhaps best practiced as a continuous habit. People think that this habit is all about closing your eyes and then trying to levitate but in reality, it is all about simply being present in the current moment. Practice feeling the present. If you're washing your hands, feel the water on your fingers. If you're eating, feel the utensils on your fingers and food in your mouth. If you're listening to someone, really listen and don't wait for your turn to speak.

It isn't an overnight fix, but you'll see changes in your behavior a lot sooner than you might expect.

Reframing

The essence of reframing comes down to believing and focusing on the fact that every cloud has a silver lining. No matter how tough you might find trading and no matter how difficult it might be for you to get results at the moment, there's always something good for you to focus on.

Losing money is an intensely emotional process and there's no easy way of dealing with this. Beginner traders are actually lucky in this regard because they come to the process without any scars. Experienced traders like yourself as not as lucky. You have prior experience when it comes to taking a devastating loss, of having done everything perfectly and then watching as your trade goes for a loss.

Perhaps one of the worst experiences in the market is when prices approach your profit levels but then miss it by a pip and then gradually and painstakingly proceed to move towards your stop loss. These experiences are what make you strong but in the heat of the moment, it just doesn't seem worth the price you have to pay to become a great trader.

You've already seen how you need to monitor your post-trade thoughts and record them. In these moments, a great practice to implement is to reframe your negative thoughts and do not let them go unchallenged. There will be all kinds of self-harming statements you will make at these times.

Here's a helpful framework for you to establish your reframing practice. In case you're wondering, these questions are used by cognitive behavioral therapists when they deal with patients who suffer from issues such as low self-esteem and constant self-doubt. Trading is a fertile ground for exposing these weaknesses in you so it's worth following this protocol:

1. Is there a huge amount of evidence substantiating your claim?
2. Is there any evidence contrary to your belief?
3. Are you assessing the situation with all the facts at your disposal?
4. What is a positive way of looking at this situation?
5. If a friend were to look at this situation what would they say? Even better, if this happened to a friend, what would you tell them with regards to this negative reaction?
6. Do you still believe your negative belief is correct and justified?

Work your way through these six questions over and over. I must warn you that it takes a lot of effort to do this. Our minds are so conditioned to beating us up and moving on that you will feel a lot of resistance when you practice this in the moment. After a losing trade, you will want to simply punch something and will want to feel that release of negativity.

The problem is that such things release physical energy, but the negative mental energy remains as it is. It simply gets embedded deeper into your subconscious and you can bet that it will rear its head at the worst possible moment for you.

Another place where these negative statements will make themselves known is during your review session. This is where you'll be looking at the things you did, right or wrong, and you're going to inevitably start wondering what was going through your head when you placed certain losing trades.

It's automatic for the brain to dial up those ingrained negative habits and to begin to curse yourself. Instead, break the pattern by following this practice. In fact, do it over and over at every single step. Brute force repetition is how the brain learns, there's just no other way. At some point in time, you're going to become aware of how your brain will walk through these questions all by itself without any prompting.

That's when you know your mind has switched over to helping you instead of hampering you.

Conclusion

So, do you feel like an advanced forex trader yet? That's a trick question. You'll never feel like one in reality. All you can do is keep working on your skills and keep trying to improve your trading edge. The word edge gets thrown around a lot in trading and many traders don't take the time to really define what it is.

Some think it's their strategy that gives them an edge. Actually, let me correct that statement. Pretty much every trader that is unsuccessful thinks the technical strategy is what constitutes an edge in trading. However, the fact is that the combination of your technical method and your risk management is what will make you money.

A significant portion of risk management is your mindset. If your brain is the tool you use to make trading decisions, it stands to reason that in order to trade well, this tool needs to be sharp. Trading with a negative mindset or a self-defeatist one is simply increasing your risk of loss in the market.

Ultimately, your greatest edge is yourself. You might have read from various trading books and educational materials that the greatest barrier to trading profits is not your strategy, but it is yourself. Well, this is because you are the one that is in full control and you happen to be your own biggest risk. The reason successful traders know themselves very well is simply that they've figured out that they are their biggest edge and managing themselves is at the forefront of everything they do.

Sure, there are risk numbers to take care of but all of this only serves to keep you on an even keel. By practicing good quantitative risk management, by risking the correct amounts and taking profits in a disciplined manner, you ensure that you will make money and this keeps you fulfilled and in a positive frame of mind in the long run.

Scaling into trading in a progressive manner helps you train your mind so that by the time you reach the live market, you're as prepared as anyone can be to tackle it. Incidentally, the scaling method that I explained in the previous book and highlighted here is how professional traders are allocated money by their employers as well. Do you really think a bank is ready to risk a million dollars on a trader before they make sure that the trader is well prepared and knows what they're doing?

Do as the pros do and you will be one. The technical system I've highlighted here is how the professionals trade the markets. The other advanced strategies here such as the carry trade and trading macros can be used successfully as well. When it comes to technical systems, there is no single correct way to trade.

However, when it comes to risk management, there are just a few practical methods to manage risk. I've highlighted the easiest of them all to implement. Follow it and you'll see that profits will follow you!

I wish you all the luck in the world with your trading efforts. Remember that you should pay attention only to the long run results. Let me know what you think of everything I have written about in this book. How has it changed your perspective on trading? I would love to hear what you have to say!

References

Chen, J. (2020). Learn About Trading FX with This Beginner's Guide to Forex Trading. Retrieved 2 April 2020, from **https://www.investopedia.com/articles/forex/11/why-trade-forex.asp**

Hall, M. (2020). 9 Forex Trading Tips. Retrieved 2 April 2020, from **https://www.investopedia.com/articles/forex/08/successful-trader-traits.asp**

Hanson, R., & Mendius, R. (2009). Buddha's brain. Oakland, CA: New Harbinger Publications.

Keupper, J. (2020). Getting started in forex. Retrieved 2 April 2020, from **https://www.investopedia.com/trading/getting-started-forex/**

Mitchell, C. (2020). Forex (FX) Definition and Uses. Retrieved 2 April 2020, from **https://www.investopedia.com/terms/f/forex.asp**

Parker, T. (2020). The Basics Of Currency Trading. Retrieved 2 April 2020, from https://www.investopedia.com/financial-edge/0412/the-basics-of-currency-trading.aspx

Made in the USA
Las Vegas, NV
26 February 2021

18621469R00094